IVY's STORY

Robin Blythe-Lord

© 2003, 2008, 2011

3rd edition 2011

For: Lesley, Zoë, Elys, Rosie, Talitha, Gareth, Bruce and Lucille

Hooe 1933 Map Key

1 Nos 1 and 2 Beach Cottages
2 Hooe School original buildings
3 Hooe School 1931 replacement building
4 St Anthony's Chapel
5 Phillips' Dairy
6 Site of 7 Fanshawe Terrace
7 Tunnel used as air raid shelter
8 Harwood's Bakery
9 Hooe House

ISBN 978-0-9541562-3-7

THANK YOU

Grateful thanks to all the following who gave of their time and support.

Zoë Blythe-Lord
Lesley Blythe-Lord
Ivy Cox, without whose memory, enthusiasm and collection of her life's records none of this would have been possible
Jake Daykin, Headteacher, Hooe School
Ralph Evans
Eddie Hunwicks
Jane Iverson, Curator Britannia Mining Museum
Steve Johnson
Ian Maxted
Brian Mosely
Chris Robinson
Paul Rogers
Debbie Watson
Local Studies staff, Plymouth Libraries

Ivy's Story

Robin Blythe-Lord

Second edition January 2008

Third edition with additions on pages 29 and 70 January 2011

© 2003 2008 2011.

All rights reserved. No part of this publication may be reproduced, stored in a retrieval system or transmitted in any form or by any means without prior permission of the copyright holder.

Published by Ateliers
Camelot, Plymouth, PL9 9RJ, UK.
Tel: 01752 403321
eMail Ivystory@ateliers.demon.co.uk

FOREWORD

This is the story of Ivy Cox, but it could be your story or anybody's story.

What I like about this book is that it is a shining example of what anyone could do with a bit of inspiration and determination. Of course it helps that Ivy has enjoyed a good long life and is possessed of a fine memory, but there is no reason why anyone, from any walk of life, couldn't attempt to compile a biography of this sort and thereby provide friends and family with an insight into those things you think they should know about you and yet perhaps you never spoken to them about before.

It matters not how seemingly ordinary your story is for there is no such thing as an ordinary story - everyone of us is different and everyone of us sees the world in a slightly different way.

Ivy's story takes us on fascinating journey through the twentieth century, reminding us of many aspects of everyday life that too many historians deem to be too specific to be of widespread interest but which are in fact the very stuff of life, like recipes, refuse, relationships and work. Through this one life story we are also treated to a potted history of the development of photography in the middle years of the twentieth century and, as with so many of the fascinating digressions contained herein, you find yourself stopping mid-page and thinking about how this relates to your own experience.

Not surprisingly perhaps, working in a photographers studio, Ivy has one or two pictures from her working days, something that not everyone can claim. It's strange isn't it, work occupies a huge amount of our time over the years and yet we often have little in the way of photographic proof to show that we ever had a job at all!

So please, take a good look at Ivy's Story and then either sit down yourself or find someone wonderful like Robin Blythe-Lord to help you record your story, even if you're still less than half-way through it! You'll find it both fun and frustrating, liberating and thought provoking and ultimately very rewarding - not just for you but for others too.

CHRIS ROBINSON

CONTENTS

Chapter 1   4
    Childhood, play and school

Chapter 2   17
    Work and marriage

Chapter 3   30
    Malta and the war

Chapter 4   42
    Post war years

Eddie's Hunwicks   47
    Boyhood memories

Appendices   54
    Washday   54
    Sewage   55
    Sloe Gin   56
    Dalmeny House   57
    Plymouth cinemas   57
    Photography   60
    RAAF   60
    HMT Dunera   61
    Nap   62
    Recipes   63
    Malta grocery list   64
    Navy food slang   64
    Paul Rogers   65
    Edwin Rogers   65
    Hooe school   66
    George Siggers   70

Index   71

CHAPTER 1
Childhood, Play and School

My Father, Herbert Henry Hunwicks, came from London and was a warrant officer in the Navy. He was stationed at Devonport when he met my mother, who was in gentleman's service.

My Mother, Caroline Emma Ann Caple Cavill, was born in Mark, East Huntspill, Somerset on the 14th September 1885. She was two when her mother died after a second child was born, who also died.

Mum's father went away, I am not sure how or why, so his parents brought Mum up. The Cavills were farmers and butchers. Mum told us of her childhood on the farm. She would ride to school on the mare, which also used to take her grandfather to market and bring him home safely after visiting several pubs! Her mother's grandfather built Heath House Farm at Foxhill, West Huntspill. Nowadays we say someone has built something even if they have just hired a builder but he actually made the bricks, fired them and laid them!

Herbert and Caroline married in 1910 and lived in rooms at 29 Avondale Terrace in Keyham, Plymouth, where I was born on the 20th August 1913. I was baptised Ivy Irene Hunwicks at St James' Church, Devonport, on the 4th September 1913.

Ivy aged 2 with her mother, Caroline, in 1915.

Avondale Terrace, Keyham in 2003. Now renumbered as Saltash Road. No29 adjoined on the right and was one of the first to be bombed during the second world war. 1 to 28 were later demolished.

My earliest recollection is being taken up to the naval barracks to see Daddy's ship going out. I had a little fur around my neck and a muff to keep my hands warm. My boots were buttoned up with button hooks. Dad was off to Malta then but he left Mum carrying another baby. He never saw that one because I had whooping cough at 18 months and the little girl caught it and she died when just a fortnight old.

In those days sailors went away for two to three years, came home for five days and away again, but usually left the wife carrying another baby.
When Dad came home from Malta he was posted

Forth Bridge looking towards South Queensferry.

to Scotland, so we left Devonport and took a little railway cottage under the Forth Bridge in South Queensferry. I well remember Mum and I walking

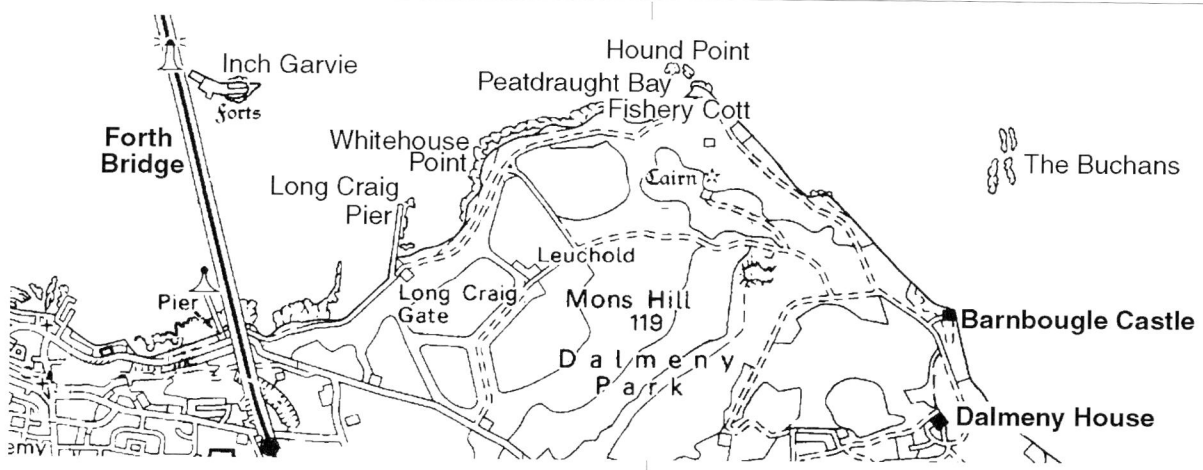

along the beach from the bridge around the point towards Barnbougle Castle, which was on Lord Rosebury's estate, part of which had been a hospital in the first world war. [>**Dalmeny House**]
On the way we used to pick mussels to eat and

Barnbougle Castle. The family home of the Earls of Rosebury until 1817, when Dalmeny House was completed.

driftwood for the fire. These little cottages were originally built for the men who painted and looked after the bridge. I can remember that our water tap was outside the front door, enclosed in a little wooden cover.

We had good times in Scotland. I can remember once Mum staying up all night to make me some dolls' clothes. It was so cold in the winter up there we had quite a lot of clothes on. I used to have a vest, then a chemise and stays, which Mum made out of flannel. We did hear of some children who had their winter clothes stitched on them and didn't dare take them off during the worst of the winter in case they caught cold.

I started school in Scotland. I can remember that the school was at the top of a little lane and we were given wooden sticks in all lovely colours to make shapes with on the desk; about the size of pencils

they were. The first world war came to an end and I can remember Armistice Day. Mum had me wrapped in a scotch shawl and we went down to the beach to watch all the ships come in, including my Dad's. People were playing cards on the pavement and everyone danced and sang.

TO HOOE

By this time I had a sister, Nellie, born in Scotland in 1918. She was five years younger than me because Dad had been away a bit longer. In 1920 Dad was posted back to Devonport. He managed, through another sailor, to get a little semi detached cottage for us in Hooe, number one Beach Cottage.
Hooe is a small village at the head of Hooe Lake,

Numbers 1 & 2 Beach Cottage in 2003.

which is a tidal inlet off the Cattewater. Numbers one and two were built by the Elford family. We were told that they were comparatively new to the rest of the houses in the village and were right up-to-date. When we lived there it consisted of a front room and a living room. The front room overlooked the lake and Dad's piano occupied most of it. The living room had a table and chairs, a food cupboard and a gas stove. We ate and did the cooking in there. There was a small recess curtained off where we washed and there were a couple of buckets in case any of us were caught short and the outside toilet was occupied. The galvanised steel bath was hung on the wall outside. There were two bedrooms upstairs. Because Dad was home all the time there were soon two brothers (Ernie and Eddie) and another sister (Betty). Next door in number two there was a family of eight, the Gales, and there was only the one toilet for both cottages in the court outside. The old wooden door never shut properly so we used to have to sing loudly to let people know there was someone in there. We each had favourite songs, Eddies was 'God Save the King', one of the Gale boys did a good impression of Bing Crosby. **[>Sewage]**

and rubbed on the rubbing board with Sunlight Soap. Everything was then boiled in the copper with washing soda. There followed three rinses in clean water, one of which had Reckitt's Blue in it, then out onto the line. She had to wait her turn to use the washing house as Mrs Gale took in soldiers' washing from the Forts. I've known her and Mum both washing out there at midnight with candles. We collected firewood from Staddon Brakes and the lake shore for the copper and the open fireplaces in the house. **[>Washday]**

Very often, especially, in the spring and autumn, the court got flooded on the spring tides. The water used to come over the quay, up through the alleyway and join up the other side where the Royal Oak

Above: Wash house at No 1 Beach Cottage in 2003. The outside toilet occupied the space on the left, between the wash house and the courtyard wall. It was removed in the 1960's when indoor facilities were provided.

Mum used to do the washing outside in the wash house. She had to light the fire under the copper, which was in the left hand back corner. Then things that had obstinate stains were scrubbed

Right: No1 Beach Cottage. Thought to have been built circa 1902.

The walls are solid and constructed from small locally quarried pieces of limestone (max size approx 300mm) which are covered with a thick cement mortar render that is grooved to suggest rectangular stonework.

In its original state the only exterior features would have been the rainwater downpipe from the centre gully and the waste water pipe from the kitchen sink. Water came from a stand pipe in the yard. The rear double bedroom has been divided to form a single bedroom with bathroom.

Hooe Lake and Village circa 1920. Number one, Beach Cottage arrowed.
The start of a timber storage raft can be seen on the right of the lake. This belonged to Bayly's timber yard at the entrance to Hooe Lake. Half way up the photograph on the left edge can be seen the ruins of St Anthony's chapel.

pub is. The quay and the road were partly raised twice but it still ran right up the road to the Post Office. We kids were always in the water and out in the middle of the lake. There were great rafts of seasoning timber from Bayly's timber yard moored around the lake and we used to swim out and sit on them. [>**Eddie**]

FOOD

The whole house was on gas for cooking and lighting, no electricity at all. Dieting was unheard of. We were fed on fat bacon, dripping, tripe and onions, bacon and onion pudding, hash-up and stews. We had home made pasties once a week. Sometimes we had a stuffed Bream baked in the oven with egg sauce. Also a lot of Toe-Rag, this was dried cod about twopence (1p) a piece. It was sometimes displayed outside shops, open to flies, dogs and goodness knows what else. We got ours from Harwoods bakery in Hooe Village, where it was kept indoors. When it had been soaked and boiled it was quite nice. Sunday's joint was often a Beef joint or half a pigs

The term 'toe-rag' comes from the 1880's and refers to strips of cloth that convicts, or prisoners of war, used to wrap around their feet because socks were unavailable. It soon became a term of abuse for anything lowly or of poor quality. In the case of the humble salt cod there was also a visual similarity!

head bought on a Saturday night down at the butchers under King Street arch. The cheek part was roasted and its ears and tongue made a stew later in the week. Dad had an allotment at the top of Hexton Hill. There was always competitions between the gardeners as to who could grow the biggest vegetables. I remember one year Arthur Gale (next door) had the biggest cabbages you ever saw and he reckoned it was because he had got a load of fish heads from the Barbican for fertilizer.

We had to mind our manners when having a sit-down meal. No playing with toys or getting down until we had all finished eating.

Breakfast

Porridge, or fried chitterlings. If we'd had tripe and onions for lunch the previous day there would sometimes be a bit of tripe left over and we'd have it fried for breakfast. Lovely that was. Eggs and bacon from the farm of course, all free range too. We didn't have a lot of toast but we'd have bread with marmalade or jam.

Lunch

We called the meal at lunch time 'Dinner'. That was always *the* large meal. Sometimes we'd have what I called 'Sticky Dinner', which was pork bones and vegetables. Mum used to make a lot of her gravy with milk so there was milk in this and a lot of parsley so it looked a bit like a white sauce. The gelatine from the bones used to make it quite thick. Then there could be Lash-Up-and-Stow or Hoosh Teegoosh. Dad used to make these, (see below). Cold cuts on Mondays of course.

Tea

This was a more hurried affair as there were seven children coming and going so it was mainly things

like apple tart and custard, jelly, cake, buns and bread and jam. You would often leave with something in your hand to eat on the way. It wasn't a sit down meal for the family.

There wasn't anything before you went to bed except possibly biscuits or a piece of bread and jam but there was always cocoa. Proper Bourneville Cocoa, it was made mainly with water because we couldn't afford the milk but that helped us to sleep.

I couldn't go to school when I came from Scotland in 1920 because Hooe St. John's School, in what is now

Hoosh Teegoosh. (Family slang. Navy slang refers to a 'hoosh' as a stew. What the 'Teegoosh' actually means is not known.)
onions, corned beef, OXO, potatoes, salt and pepper, water.

Place chopped onions in a baking dish and sprinkle with OXO cube, salt and pepper and a breakfast cup of water.
Cut slices of corned beef and place on the onion. Cover with sliced or mashed potatoes and bake for about an hour on gas mark 5 or 190°C.

Lash up and Stow
Self raising flour, suet, bacon, onion, salt and pepper.

Make a suet dough with 1lb of self raising flour and 8ozs of suet mixed with a little water.
Roll out into a sheet and cover with chopped bacon and onion. Add salt and pepper to taste. Roll it up like a swiss roll in a baking cloth and tie up, hence the name as it looked a bit like a rolled up hammock. Boil for 1 1/2 to 2 hours. Slice and serve.
[>**Recipes**]

TO SCHOOL

St. John's Church Hall, was a hospital and there were still a lot of wounded soldiers in there from the first world war. Plymstock was the next nearest which Mum said was too far for me to go. She would wait for Hooe School to re-open as this was going to happen quite soon. Consequently I was getting on for seven before I started school again but even then we didn't get much education as there were so many teachers coming and going. I can remember Miss England who sat on a very high chair with a cane in her hand and she terrified all of us. Then

Incidentally we also had a lot of Roman Catholic children in our school, they were soldiers' children from Fort Bovisand. We wouldn't think of rowing with them over their religion, everyone was treated the same. The only difference was that they brought sandwiches for lunch whereas we could get home.

I remember once we were sitting in class and there was thunder. A pupil put her hand up shouting "Miss, Miss, there's a ball of fire!" but before the teacher realised what was happening it burst

Hooe School 1925 or 26. See page 70

1 Daisy Ford
2 ? Demelweek
3 Irene Axworthy
4 George Strudwick?
5 Ted Sallows
6 ? Burridge
7 Lily Roberts
8 Nellie Atkins
9 ?
10 Stan Edgecombe
11 ?
12 George Siggers
13 Harry Watts?
14 Ivy Hunwicks
15 Ivy Atkins
16 Hilma Glynn
17 Ivy Tucker
18 ?
19 ? Pascoe
20 George Duncan
21 ? Brown
22 Reg Tucker
23 Lloyd Body
24 Tom Jacman
25 George Pearse
26 Harold Pascoe

Photograph taken in the girl's playground against the road wall

quite a nice head teacher came but there was a lot of violence even then. I remember an unruly boy throwing a pen at him and the nib stuck in his face. He didn't stay long. Then there was a Frenchman took over, he was a bit touchy strokey with the girls, he didn't last long either.

It wasn't until Mr and Mrs Rogers came that we really learned anything, their son was Paul Rogers, the actor. [>**Paul Rogers, Edwin Rogers**]

through the woodwork at the side of the high up windows in the roof and wood splintered all over our desks. No-one was hurt, it was just like pieces of coal. Our parents were worried because they had seen it hit the school from the village. All it meant to us was that we didn't have to go back to school after dinner. [>**School**]

THE MILK ROUND

I couldn't wait for the school day to end because

Hooe School circa 1923 Class 1

1 Mr Edwin Rogers (Headmaster)
2 Harry Gilpin
3 Bobby Vokes
4 Cyril Thomas
5 ?
6 Tom Gray
7 Robert Duncan
8 George Gray
9 ? Gill
10 ? Atwill
11 Herbert Skilton
12 Zena Walton
13 Susy Lebraun
14 ?
15 ?
16 Iris Skilton
17 ?
18 Kath Charlick?
19 ?
20 Ivy Vokes
21 Ivy Hunwicks
22 Dorothy Hughes
23 Amy Dale
24 Nellie Sallows
25 Phil Pascoe
26 ?
27 Dorothy Holloway
28 Turner or Robins
29 ?
30 Joyce Hine
31 Eileen Thomas
32 ?
33 Bessie Dungey
34 ?
35 Ivy Lillicrap
36 Vanny Gray
37 Roy Cockrell
38 Arthur Parnell
39 ? Skilton
40 Dick Skilton
41 ? Glinn
42 ?
43 Paul Rogers (Headmaster's son)
44 Hedley Doddridge
45 Albert Pearse
46 Sydney Saunders

Photograph taken in the boy's playground against the school wall

The staff of a typical farm and dairy of the area circa 1905. The equipment, methods and conditions would have remained very similar up to 1950.

I was about ten now. I took the milk around for Hines. They had the dairy and Post Office just up the hill from the Victoria Inn. I used to do it before and after school, take about 12 cans at a time on my fingers around the village of Lower Hooe. The furthest was the Revells' house. I used to go up Hexton Hill through Hooe village, over the stile at the top and down over the allotments. At the bottom of the allotments there was a gate. You went through the gate and up through a little garden to Revell's House on the right. Every Saturday Mrs Revell used to give me tuppence (two old pennies, one new penny) with which I could buy 1/4lb (110 grams) of toffee. I got 2/6d (12.5p) for the weeks' milk round and 1/3d (6.25p) for helping in the dairy on a Saturday morning. By this time I was glad to put a bit of money in Mum's hand as Dad had come out of the navy and couldn't find any work.

Hooe School 1920's Class 2 sister Nellie's class

1 Miss Knott. (Married Mr Smale)
2 ?
3 ? Tugwell
4 Paul Rogers
5 Stan Oats
6 ? Gray?
7 Bobby Vokes
8 Arthur Oxland
9 Ernie Williams
10 ?
11 ?
12 ?
13 Kathleen Dale
14 Edie Jackman
15 Josie Williams
16 Vera Hughes
17 Phyllis Slocombe
18 Madalene Ralph
19 Ivy Lillicrap
20 ?
21 ?
22 Marjorie Fisher
23 ?
24 Muriel Holloway
25 ? Skilton
26 Nellie Hunwicks
27 ?
28 Audrey Woods
29 ?
30 Joan Allen
31 Melita Drake
32 ?
33 Ivy Drake
34 Joan Diamond
35 Bella Roberts
36 ?
37 M. Appleby
38 Audrey Salter
39 ?
40 Arthur Pearse
41 Clifford Oxland
42 Rodney Berry
43 ?
44 Gordon Whitefield

Photograph taken in the boy's playground against the school wall

I remember when I used to go down through the allotments to deliver Revell's milk there was a large yacht out in the lake which belonged to a Captain Barnes. He was known to have been with Scott at one time on his expedition. He started to leave boxes of chocolates for me on the gate at the bottom of the allotments and when he went to France once he sent me a present. I was invited on his yacht but I never went as I was getting old enough to be wary of him. He may have been just a kind man but Mum was getting worried too...

There was a short cut to get back to the dairy. It was through the tunnel in the quarry at the bottom of the allotments out into Hine's field at the Victoria Inn. I used to use it although I was frightened when I got into the darkness of the middle. I would rattle the cans all the way through until I saw the light at the other end. It was later used as an air raid shelter during world war two.

I made a little more pocket money by collecting people's medicines from the doctors at Plymstock.

Hooe School circa 1925

1 Frank Furse
2 George Strudwick
3 Stan Edgecombe
4 Ted Sallows
5 George Siggers
6 Tom Higgins
7 Eva Dungey
8 Vi Sayers
9 May Skilton
10 Gwen Rowse
11 Frank Rowse
12 George Grey
13 Edie Wells
14 Ivy Tucker
15 Hilma Glynn
16 May Thomas
17 Betty Rogers
18 Ivy Hunwicks
19 Ernie McInernie
20 Ivy Vokes
21 George Brown
22 Herbert Skilton
23 Wilfrid England
24 Albert Brown
25 Walter Gale
26 Harold Gale
27 Terrence McInernie
28 ? Brown
29 Jack Urell
30 John Tugwell
31 Tom Grey
32 Fred Tucker
33 Marjorie Oats
34 Ivy Skilton
35 Jack Gale
36 Amy Salmon
37 Elsie Charlick
38 Rene Mansell
39 Nellie Atkins
40 May Orchard
41 Irene Jolliffe
42 Kath Charlick
43 Linda Kurnow
44 Vi Tugwell
45 Emily Gale
46 Lily Dungey
47 Linda Curnow
48 ? Vokes
49 Ivy Atkins
50 Lily Roberts
51 Nellie Sayers
52 Philys Tiller
53 Mr Edwin Rogers
   (Headmaster)
54 Miss Knott
55 Alice Young
56 Florrie Pape
57 Ena Ball
58 - Pascoe
59 Elsie Gilpin
60 Bill Salmon
61 Clifford Sparks
62 Lloyd Body
63 George Grey
64 Tom Jackman
65 George Duncan
66 Cyril Thomas
67 Reg Tucker
68 Dick Skilton

Photograph taken in the girl's playground against the school entrance

We used to go from Hooe School to Plymstock about once a week for cookery lessons and I would always call in at the surgery to see if there were any deliveries for Hooe. We thought nothing of walking three miles or so in those days. Sometimes we got a lift home on the coal cart. We used to sit up there and eat whatever we had made at cookery or dip our fingers in cocoa and sugar or sherbet or lemon crystals.

> The sherbet sweet powder is made from highly flavoured sugar crystals and ascorbic acid. This dissolves on the tongue to give an ice-melting effect. Real sherbets are very like sorbets and made from real fruit, finely crushed ice and a little gelatine.

We used to collect jam jars too, we got some nice toffees for those. A van used to come into the square in Hooe Village. He'd got a bucket of Macintosh or Palm toffees and would give us toffees for jam jars. They were cleaned and re-used as jars. Most bottles had refundable deposits on them too.

Bovisand circa 1935. A Stuart Postcard.

CHILDHOOD HIGHLIGHTS

1st of May. That was when we used to go around house to house with our May Queen. I was the May Queen one year and Mum made me a dress with white net over it and bunches of real violets around the bottom. There was always a bit of competition amongst the different groups to try and get up to Colonel Coates' house first (Belle View). We used to sing:

"Here comes a merry merry month of May.
Happy happy all are we
Our Queen is the best in the town
And a happy little girl is she."

They might give a 1/- (5p) or even 2/6 (12.5p)!

Bovisand Quay circa 1920. Trippers waiting to board ferries for Plymouth and the Breakwater.

The next highlight was the Sunday School outing when we used to go on the train to Yealmpton or Bere Alston tea gardens. We usually arrived there with a bit of smut or cinder in our eyes as we had been looking out of the train windows. There would be a lovely tea laid out, puff cakes with jam and cream were the favourites. After tea was best of all when the races started and you competed against one another. Vi Tucker, my friend at the time and I used to practice the three legged race for weeks before the outing and always reckoned on winning a threepenny piece (just over 1p) each and there was always the swings! I usually had my brothers and sisters to look after as well and sometimes one or the other would be sick or get hit with a swing but we were all so happy.

We were very lucky throughout the summer as we could walk to Jennycliff or better still to Bovisand, because it had the better beach. There used to be streams of people getting off the Turnchapel train and making their way to the beaches. Everything had to be carried by hand: teapot, kettle, cups, plates and saucers etc.

At Bovisand we never took water because you could fill up your kettle from the stream running down onto the beach. We picked watercress while we were there and done it up in bundles so we could sell it. Blackberries too. There seemed to be billions of sloes down the path leading to Dinson Beach. We picked them for people to make Sloe Gin.

[>Sloe Gin]

Another thing we used to do was pick winkles and take them home to boil up and pick out with a hair pin. The place we used to get the biggest and best was on the sewerage pipe running down Dinson Beach, which is the beach immediately next to Jennycliff, towards Plymouth. It would be frowned on today but we never came to any harm. In fact we used to

Vi Tucker and Ivy.

The Hunwicks at Hexton Woods circa 1926
Left to right
Front row: Nell, Ernie, Eddie
Back Row: Ivy's Father, Mother holding Betty, Ivy.

swim with it all around us. I think it is the other pollutants causing the trouble because the sea cleans natural waste.

In the summer evenings we used to make a shrimp net out of a sack and a hoop from a beer barrel or the rim of a cycle wheel. We would stitch the sack across the hoop and tie three strings to it to meet the hauling line in the middle. We would put a fish head or dead crab on the sack, weight it with a stone and lower it into the water off the wall by Turnchapel Station. You'd wait for about two minutes or so then pull it up quick. The water pressure would press the prawns into the net on the way up but you had to be quick lifting them out of the water and onto the wall else they'd jump out. We would sit for hours there catching shrimps and prawns.

I had a friend, Rene Jolliffe, who had a rowing boat so sometimes we would row out to one of the barges moored off Frosts Corner, as we called it, just the other side of the railway bridge on the way out to the Cattewater. We caught flat fish and whiting from there. The barges were used as coal stores for the Turnchapel Ferry and had a lot of weed under them. The shelter attracted fish.

Often in the autumn I used to hurry out of school in the dinner hour because the Miss Nelders, who lived in a big house opposite Belleview Hill, used to throw windfall apples out from their orchard into the field. Fanshawe Terrace wasn't built then, it was all fields. The Miss Nelders' house would be where No1 Fanshawe Terrace is now. It was a wonderful feeling to see a nice heap of apples there that I could take home to the family.

The next thing we looked forward to was Guy Fawkes Night. We made up our guy and around the houses we went singing...

"Guy Guy Guy, hit him in the eye
Stick him on a lamppost and there let him die.
If you haven't got a penny a ha'penny will do
If you haven't got a ha'penny, God Bless You."

The money we collected was spent on fireworks, bread, pickles and cheese. We headed up the Brakes to light our bonfire and let off the fireworks which the whole village could see.

Some evenings we played out around the village. "Eeek, Squeek, Me, Hallo." that meant you hid and shouted and the others had to find you. We also played paper chase, hop scotch, and marbles. I always had a bag of marbles which we played in the gutter coming home from school.

Toys and games circulated in sort of seasons, we'd play with one for a while then something else would take its place. There was the top season when we would crayon or chalk a design onto the the top and whip it around the square outside Harwoods bakery. You could have battles with those, trying to knock the other tops away and stop them spinning.

Then came hoops. You could go quite a long way beating the hoop along or putting it around your waist and seeing how long you could keep it going. We would spend hours playing skipping together, seeing who could jump the highest. Bouncing a ball against the Royal Oak wall, playing rounders.

All these needed very little equipment and hardly any expense but gave us great fun!

We used to play up in Hexton Woods too. There we might meet some of the children of the Onion family. They lived in Radford Castle, the folly built on the dam at the end of Hooe Lake. The dam controlled the water into and out of Radford Duckponds, which had been built as a source of food and recreation for Radford House.

I was getting up to fourteen years old then when you could leave school. Mum and Dad thought it was best for me to stay on an extra year as I had missed out when starting school. I was also allowed a new bike which I paid 2/8 (15p) a week for at Snells. From then on, once I mastered riding the thing, I biked everywhere. One of the first long distance runs for me was when Mum was expecting my youngest sister Betty. I had to ride up to Plymstock and get the Midwife. I arrived panting and blowing saying "Will you come quickly as Mum has had the pains." The midwife then got on her bike and rode to Hooe. She used to amuse the children as she was a huge woman on this upright bike although she told us she was only 3lbs when born.

By this time we weren't all that well off as Dad still couldn't find any regular work. He tried but because he had been in the signals in the Navy he did not have a trade that was of any use outside the Navy.

He bought a ladder and some brushes and went window cleaning, chimney sweeping and drain cleaning at Mount Batten. He was a barber for the village children, did shoe repairs and was a Devon County football referee and chairman of Hooe St. John's football club. He also used to go to Winnicotts Warehouse in Ebrington Street, it was at the town end, what is now Eastlake Street. He would buy a few dresses, housecoats and aprons and take them round door to door.

Mum never went to work. There wasn't enough work for the men and they were supposed to be the bread winners. We were a lot better off than others though because Dad had a pension from his twenty-four years in the Navy. It was paid monthly and we all used to go out to Devonport with him when he drew it. One reason for this was to make sure he didn't spend any of it on the way home! Another was that we used to get kitted out with new outfits from Tozers in Fore Street. They were cheaper there than anywhere else. Then we walked to Phoenix Wharf, just past the Barbican, to catch the ferry back to Turnchapel.

Radford Castle circa 1910.
The Sheer Legs and chutes are for loading stone from Radford Quarry (behind) into the waiting sailing barges. The stone came out in trucks on a narrow gauge tramway.

Turnchapel and Oreston Ferry. At Phoenix Wharf...

at Turnchapel Pier...

and at Oreston. This photograph circa 1930.

Being the eldest of five I was always worried about Mum. Once we got off the ferry and she dropped her purse. Several coins dropped through the landing stage into the water. As a family treat we used to go to the Grand or the Palace Theatre in Union Street. Once we queued up for ages only to be told at the box office "Sorry. No babes in arms." Mum always semed to have had one of those.

About this time they were thinking about starting a bus service from Plymouth to Hooe. There was competition between the Eddystone buses and the Palace Saloon. The young Harry Hines was a driver for the Eddystone and a family friend.

I went around to get a petition signed for him. I think in the end they both did different routes. The Eddystone colours were blue and white and the Palace Saloon was plum purple. They had a little blonde clippie who had a very smart uniform.

Its 1928 and I am coming up to fifteen and thinking seriously about leaving school and what I should do for a job. My dad sat hours with me writing letters for jobs. I sat the Co-op exam but didn't get in there. Then mum saw in the paper where some dress making firm would take on apprentices if you would pay a premium of £100 or so. This was Clarks in Lockyer Street. I went there on a months' trial. I enjoyed learning about the sewing but on talking to a couple of girls who had been there a while I decided that my parents were going to waste their money. It wasn't long after this that the firm went bankrupt.

During this time I got interested in Hooe Baptist Chapel. All my social life was taken up then by me having joined the Girls' Life Brigade and The Christian Endeavour, held on a Tuesday evening. A Miss Rosevere used to take us for sewing, knitting, knot tying, first aid, scripture, raffia work etc. We did concerts and sung things like Ole Joe, with our arms getting longer.

Mr Berry.

If I worked hard enough to get certificates for these things as well as swimming I could win prizes by taking part in the Turnchapel and Barbican Regatta. I won a book at school for writing the best composition: 'Hygiene and the Fly.'

The Superintendent was Mr Berry, he came from Plymouth and was only about twenty or so and we all fell in love with him.

We also had The City Mission Band come to the chapel. Things were never the same after they came because I started to fall in love with one or two of those bandsmen, especially the French Horn player, Bill Browne. This band was run by the Welsh brothers who ran a clothing business in Portland Square. Quite a lot of people in the village bought clothes from them on hire purchase. In fact I do not know how we would have managed without them. they were a lovely Christian family and I went around with that band to several churches in the city. It went on to become the City Silver Band.

I had a friend, Ivy Vokes, who lived in the army married quarters at Bovisand and whenever we

Motto:
"Walk in the light."—1 John 1, 7.
Still will I strive to be,
As if thou wast with me:
Whatever path I take,
It shall be for thy sake.
Thoreau
With Hearty Greetings and Sincere
Good wishes from
The Girls' Life Brigade.

The National Sunday School Union
Scripture Examination · March 1931
SUBJECT: "JESUS, THE KING."
Class Lower Senior Division
Certificate of Merit
Awarded by
Plymouth, Devonport and District
Sunday School Union
To
of Sunday School
President: REV. WALTER ROSE, B.A.
Examiner: REV. T. ELSS
General Secretary: JOHN H. BOX
Examination Secretary: E. ARCHD. EDGCOMBE

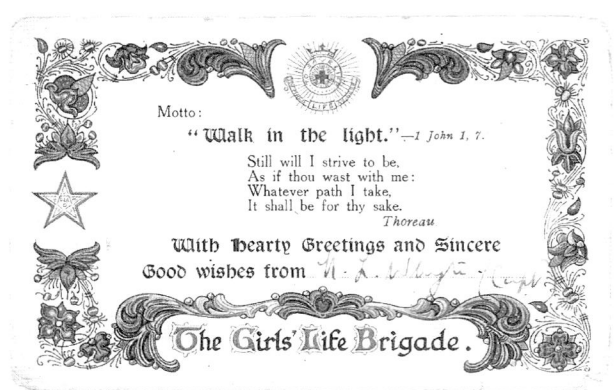

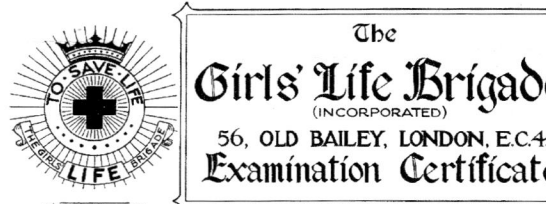

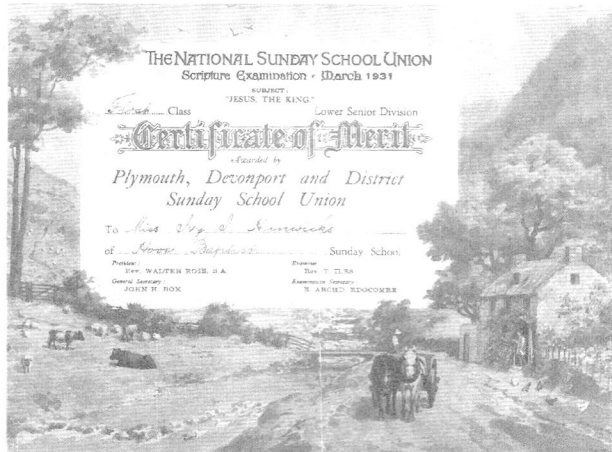

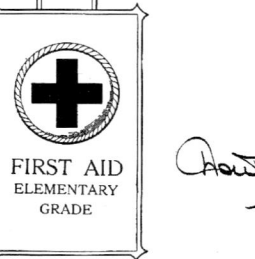

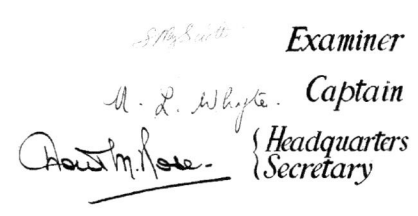

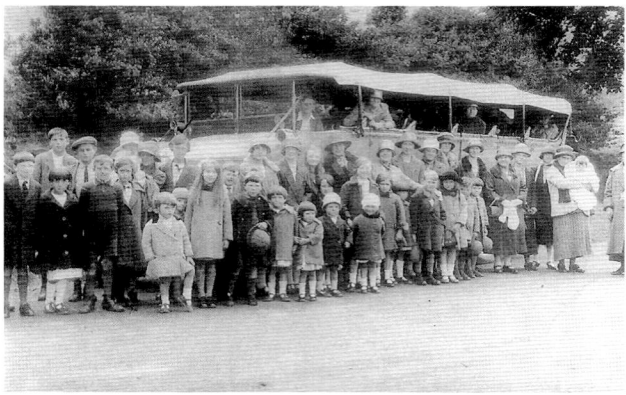

Hooe Chapel Outing probably mid 1920's though this type of bus was in use up to the mid 1930's.

There was rivalry between the Chapel and the Church, especially in the matter of outings and the respective merits of each destination. The Chapel went by charabanc to Bigbury while the Church went by train to Bere Alston, leaving from Turnchapel Station and changing at Friary in Plymouth. Of course many children went on both.

visited each other I would walk up over Staddon with her and see her go down the hill to Bovisand and she did the same for me when I visited her. This used to happen quite late in the evening and both forts, Stamford and Staddon, were full of soldiers. We had nothing to be afraid of.

TO SAVE LIFE
THE GIRLS' LIFE BRIGADE
The
Girls' Life Brigade
(INCORPORATED)
56, OLD BAILEY, LONDON, E.C.4.
Examination Certificate
This is to Certify that
Ivy Hunwick a member of the
1st Hooe Company
was examined in the under-mentioned subject and passed the required tests
Examiner
M. L. Whyte Captain
Headquarters Secretary
Date
FIRST AID
ELEMENTARY
GRADE

Devon County Education Committee.
Swimming Certificate.
This is to Certify that IVY HUNWICKS
a Pupil of the PLYMSTOCK HOOE School, passed a Test
in Swimming in the year 1928, covering a distance of 440 yards.
Chairman of Education Committee.
Superintendent of Test.
Head Teacher of School.
Date 1928.

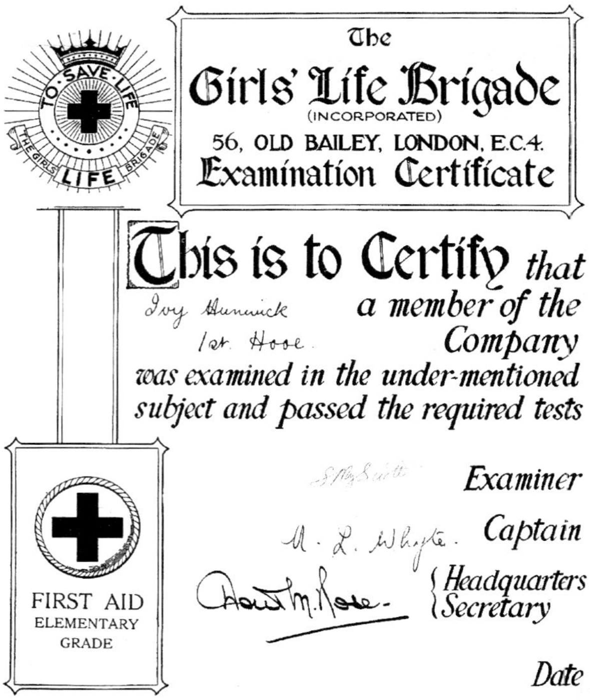

I had another friend, Edie Roberts and we used to walk a lot around Jennycliff and Mount Batten.

If we met any soldiers they always respected us girls and if they got a bit close "No!" always meant 'No' and they respected that. We learned the difference between right and wrong through our religious upbringing at the chapel and also at school which always started assembly with a hymn and prayers.

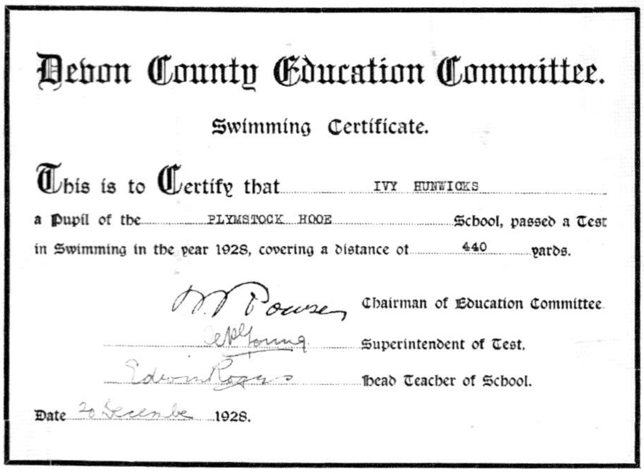

But school was finishing for me now. The end of the summer term was approaching and I would have to find a job.

CHAPTER 2
Work and Marriage

It is now 1928, I am fifteen and leaving school. I want to help bring some money into the family. At that time a skilled man would get a wage of £2 to £3 per week, while an unskilled worker got under a pound.

GOULDS

Meanwhile I toured all the shops in Plymouth to ask if they would take me on. I did get a job in Goulds, the ex-army surplus store. Their main shop was in Treville Street at the time but they opened another one, more like a bazaar, in Union Street next to the Savoy cinema. It was a very long narrow shop and we had a gramophone playing to get the customers in. We sold ladies stockings at 4d (2p) a pair. I got 5 shillings (25p) a week. Then I got promoted to the Flora Street shop as manageress at 6 shillings (30p) a week. There was only one other girl there besides me, Dorothy Bray. We used to have a lot of war damaged clothing such as long johns and vests. Some of it had blood and wound holes in it. We had to sort it all out and sell the best. I think I lasted about six months there as the Goulds were very hard taskmasters. They also seemed to quarrel with each other all the time.

Goulds in Ebrington Street. 2003.
Still selling their famous exWD stock this shop has occupied the premises of the Cinedrome Cinema since the early 1950's and is now their only branch.
Treville Street was at the town end of Ebrington Street, under what is now Eastlake Walk and the Drake Circus complex so the shop is very close to the original site.

One instance: Mrs Gould would put a cap on a stand, add a 'For Sale' ticket to it and place it on the counter. Mr Gould would come into the shop, see the cap and knock it off the counter saying "What the hell is that doing there?"

There used to be a coal cart come down Flora Street some days. Taylor's from Desborough Road. Bill Taylor used to call in and see us girls sometimes. It was alright until one evening he came into the shop to show off his Scout uniform when Mr Gould came in. I tried to pretend Bill was buying something but it didn't work. You see we weren't suppose to talk to anyone unless they were a customer and then, bar pleasantries, we should only talk about the purchase. We were both sacked and I was manageress at the time. 1929 that was.

STUARTS PHOTO SERVICES

Then Dorothy and I saw that Stuart's Photo Services in Notte Street were advertising for darkroom workers. We went down and Mr. Bailey took us on. It was a photo processing factory belonging to George and Jack Bailey of Geoffrey Stuart's, 110 Union Street. Jack was manager of the factory. The only snag was that you started in April and the season finished in September, so you had to find a winter job.

Artisan Dwellings were on the South side of Notte Street, between Hoe Street and Hoegate Street. Just off the left hand side of the picture is Hoegate Street. This photograph, date unknown, was taken from across the road where St. Andrew Street joins Notte Street.

There was a large enclosed courtyard through the arch. Stuarts had labs on left as you went in and on the right was Varcoe's furniture store. In the central part, under the overhanging windows, was a sweet shop. Most of the rest of the building was private flats. The building was severely damaged during the war and demolished soon afterwards in Plymouth's spate of regeneration. Hoe Approach was driven through the site of the arch and courtyard.

I loved it there through the summer. I was able to have my lunch at Dorothy's house in Hoegate Street as Stuart's was in the Artisan Dwellings in Notte Street. You went through an arch off Notte Street, just up from Hoegate street. Inside it was

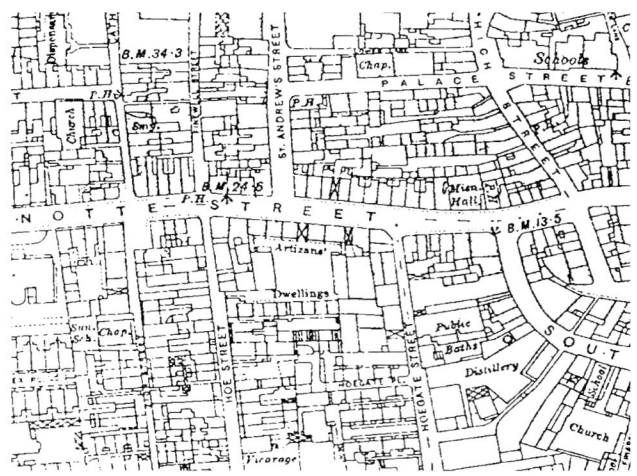
Notte Street and Artisan's Dwellings. Circa 1893.

a large square with houses or works all around. There had been a brewery in there. [Notte Street Brewery]. There was a furnishing company on the right and ahead of you were houses, Stuart's had all the left hand side. We used to come out and buy sweets in one of the shops outside in Notte Street during our dinner hour.

Lady Astor came up into Artisan Dwellings Square canvassing from the back of a lorry. There was always a good argument, or heckling match, from Barbican folk. She was very popular though. The MP Michael Foote's family lived on the corner of Notte Street and Hoegate Street, I think his father Isaac had an engineering business there.

Lady Astor and family at Cliveden.
On the reverse:
Printed: Best Wishes from all the Astors. Cliveden 1922
Handwritten: Lady Nancy with the family when I first joined the Astors. Property of R Harrison.

L to R: Lady Nancy Astor, Mr R S Shaw (first Son), Mr Billy Astor, Miss Wissie, Mr David, Michael and Jakie (sic)

There was no National Health Service in those days. I remember Mum kneeling down in front of the fire with terrible toothache and couldn't afford to go to the dentist. I paid for her to have her teeth out and get a new set because I got a bit of compensation because of a cycling accident in 1929.

What happened was my friend Edie and I were coming down Stentaway Road on our bikes. We were approaching the junction with Billacombe Road and there were workmen building Mumford's Garage [now Fairway Furniture] on the left. They started wolf whistling as we passed. Two sixteen year olds, well... We followed each other out onto the main road and a car came between us. My friend Edie nearly got across and just sat down in the road. I caught the worst of it and finished up in hospital with a broken ankle and concussion. We were probably in the wrong but I couldn't remember anything and apparently the man in the car had 'another woman' in it and so settled out of court. Edie got £18 and I got £31. I was rich enough to pay for my Mums' teeth to be done.

After all that she never wore them, mainly because they were so big and clumsy. She could eat anything without her teeth and actually looked better without them.

Edie and Ivy with their bicycles after the accident.

The photo girls at Stuarts.
Taken in the Artisan Dwellings courtyard, outside the door to Stuarts. Circa 1930

1 Myrtle ?	9 Unknown	17 Edna Blackner
2 Millie Hooper	10 A French Girl	18 Emily Wilcocks
3 Dorothy Bray	11 Unknown	19 Unknown
4 Elsie Parker	12 Gladys Clatworthy	20 Miss Vickerstaff
5 Cissie Piper	13 Alfie Lecount	21 Miss Pullen
6 Hilda Brimacombe.	14 Unknown	22 Carrie Carve
7 Lena Austin	15 Ivy Hunwicks	23 Unknown
8 Ivy Hoskins	16 May McAuliffe	

Stuarts used to process films that were handed in to chemists, their own photos from the studio in Union Street and they also took and printed a wide range of local postcards. The two of us were developing films in deep red light. The darkroom consisted of six 40 gallon (151.5 litres) tanks. The first was filled with developer, the second a stop bath, three and four were fixing and five and six were washes.

We would unroll the film and place a clip at each end. The clip slid over a rod that held six films. When I first went there we had to place each rod individually by hand into the developer, stop bath and so on. Then one day Mr Bayley introduced an overhead wire track, a bit like the tracks that carried money to the cashiers in big stores, or a ski chair lift. It was strung over the line of tanks and attached to this were cages that held 10 rods of films. We were able to pull the whole cage along the wires by an arm then lower it down into the developer tank then up and out, along and down into the wash and so on. It was alright as long as the cage didn't tilt. If it did the rods would fall out and you would lose all the films down the bottom of the tank. You would have to prod about with a long pole hoping to fish them out and being careful not to dig and scratch the soft film emulsion.

The time through each tank was important for the process to be completed properly and we had

THE BALDAX SERIES

Give 4 × 6 cm. results. 16 exposures on standard 8-exp. 3¼ × 2¼ Roll Film. Beautifully finished. Self-erecting movement. Camera opens ready for immediate use. Very sturdy construction.
MODEL I.
F/4.5 Trioplan Anastigmat, Pronto Shutter speeded 1/25,1/50 & 1/100 sec., T. and B. Brilliant direct finder, focussing from 5ft. to infinity. **£4 7 6**
MODEL II.
F/3.5 Trioplan Anastigmat, Ibsor Everset Sector shutter with D.A. adjustment. Speeds 1 to 1/150 sec. T. and B. General specification as Model I. **£5 7 6**
MODEL III.
F/3.5 Trioplan Anastigmat, Compur Sector Shutter speeded 1-1/300 sec. T. and B., general specification as Model I .. **£6 6**
THE PICCOCHIC RANGE.
Giving 16 3 × 4 cm. photographs on standard 8 exp. V.P. film. Genuine F/2.9 Meyer Trioplan Anastigmat, Compur Sector shutter speeded 1-1/300 sec., T. and B., focussing adjustment from infinity to 3 ft. Complete in pocket case **£6 5**
Other models available.
Any of above on 7 days' approval against full deposit.

"N & G" SIBYLS

"New Special" & "Baby"

Are the small cameras that appeal to those who appreciate exquisite workmanship and excellent photographs.

There are no cameras that will do just what the "Sibyls" can. The sweetness of the "Sibyl" shutters will enable quarter-second exposures to be made whilst holding the camera in the hand—the "Sibyl" shutter speeds are guaranteed accurate and there is no "kick" in its use.

"NEW SPECIAL" SIBYL

For Plates $3\frac{1}{2} \times 2\frac{1}{2}$ or Film Packs $3\frac{1}{4} \times 2\frac{1}{4}$ or for Roll-films $3\frac{5}{8} \times 2\frac{5}{16}$. High Precision shutter with speeds to 1/150 sec. including $\frac{1}{2}$, $\frac{1}{4}$ and $\frac{1}{8}$ sec. Focussing by lever with well separated scale, depth of field scale on lever, folding reflector or direct vision finder, full rising and cross front, sliding metal lens hood, Ross Xpres and Dallmeyer Serrac F 4.5 anastigmat.

BABY "SIBYL"

For Plates or Film Packs $4\frac{1}{2} \times$ 6cm. or for Roll-films $2\frac{5}{8} \times 1\frac{5}{8}$. Similar specification to above, excepting shutter speeded to 1/200 sec. and depth of field scale omitted. Direct vision finder only on Plate and Film Pack model.

Send for illustrated catalogue of all "N & G" models—post free.

NEWMAN & GUARDIA LTD.

63, NEWMAN STREET, OXFORD STREET, LONDON, W.1

Telegrams: Goniometer, Rath, London.

Telephone: Museum 1081.

LONDON'S LEADING DEALERS in GOOD *Second-Hand* CAMERAS

A SELECTION FROM OUR STOCK.

$4\frac{1}{4} \times 3\frac{1}{4}$ Adams Vesta, $5\frac{1}{4}$in. Ross F/4.5 Xpres lens, shutter speeds 1 to 1/300th sec., Adams patent view finder, changing box for 8 plates, Mackenzie adapter, 12 envelopes, leather case, in good condition **£9 17 3**

$4\frac{1}{4} \times 3\frac{1}{4}$ Junior Model Sanderson, $5\frac{1}{2}$in. Beck F/6 Convertible Bystigmar lens, Universal shutter, speeds 1 to 1/250th sec., 3 double plate-holders, filmpack-holder, leather case, in excellent condition **£9 12 6**

$3\frac{1}{2} \times 2\frac{1}{2}$ N. & G. New Special Sibyl, Ross F/4.5 Xpres lens, also 9in. Dallon F/6.5 Telephoto lens, 3 double plate-holders, filmpack-holder, leather case, in good condition ... **£19 10 0**

$4\frac{1}{4} \times 3\frac{1}{4}$ Sinclair Una, double extension, revolving back, 5in. Ross Zeiss F/6.3 Convertible Protar lens, Compound shutter, speeds 1 to 1/250th sec., 4 double plate-holders, leather case, in excellent condition **£12 10 0**

$3\frac{1}{2} \times 2\frac{1}{2}$ Sands Hunter Universal, brass-bound teak body, double extension, revolving back, 4in. Ross F/5.5 Combinable lens, Lukos Express shutter, speeds 1 to 1/300th sec., 3 double bookform plate-holders, filmpack-holder, leather case, in good condition........... **£12 10 0**

$3\frac{1}{2} \times 2\frac{1}{2}$ N. & G. New Special Sibyl, Ross F/4.5 Xpres lens, N. & G. Reflex finder, 3 double plate-holders, filmpack-holder, leather case, in good condition **£13 10 0**

4.5 × 6 cm. N. & G. Baby Sibyl, Zeiss F/4.5 Tessar lens, also $5\frac{1}{2}$in. Dallon F/6.5 Telephoto lens, 3 double plate-holders, filmpack-holder, leather case, good condition **£13 10 0**

$3\frac{1}{2} \times 2\frac{1}{2}$ Soho Reflex, revolving back, double extension, Ross F/3.5 Xpres lens, 3 double plate-holders, in brand new condition. List price **£35.** For **£25 0 0**

$4\frac{1}{4} \times 3\frac{1}{4}$ T.P. Ruby de Luxe Reflex, revolving back, 6in. Dallmeyer F/2.9 Pentac lens, 3 double plate-holders, filmpack-holder, canvas case. List price **£35.** For **£17 12 6**

$4\frac{1}{4} \times 3\frac{1}{4}$ Tropical Soho Reflex, revolving back, $5\frac{1}{4}$in. Ross F/4.5 Xpres lens, 6 double plate-holders, leather case, in excellent condition. List price **£45.** For **£27 12 6**

$4\frac{1}{4} \times 3\frac{1}{4}$ Soho Reflex, revolving back, double extension, 6in. Dallmeyer F/2.9 Pentac lens, 3 double plate-holders, filmpack-holder, leather case, in excellent condition. List price over **£40.** For **£24 16 6**

$3\frac{1}{2} \times 2\frac{1}{2}$ N. & G. Folding Reflex, Ross F/2.9 Xpres lens, 2 N. & G. changing boxes for cut films, film-pack-holder, leather case, in practically new condition. List price **£70.** For **£36 12 6**

$5\frac{1}{2} \times 3\frac{1}{2}$ Postcard Tropical Soho Reflex, $6\frac{1}{2}$in. Ross F/4.5 Xpres lens, filmpack-holder, changing box, leather case, in good condition... **£21 10 0**

$3\frac{1}{4} \times 2\frac{1}{4}$ Ensign Rollfilm Reflex, 4in. Dallmeyer F/4.5 Anastigmat lens, also 9in. Dallmeyer F/6.5 Telephoto lens, self-capping focal plane shutter, speeds 1/25th to 1/500th sec., leather carrying case, in new condition. List price **£20.** ....For **£13 12 6**

4.5 × 6 cm. Baby Soho Reflex, revolving back, quick-wind self-capping focal plane shutter, 4in. Cooke Series II A F/3.5 lens, 3 double plate-holders, filmpack-holder, leather case, in excellent condition. List price **£35 12 6.** For **£22 10 0**

$3\frac{1}{4} \times 2\frac{1}{4}$ Adams Verto, for roll-films and plates, double extension, 4in. Ross F/5.5 Combinable Anastigmat lens, shutter speeds 1 to 1/250 sec., 3 double plate-holders, single lenses 7in. focus, filmpack-holder, hooded focussing screen, lens hood and leather case, in good condition. Original price **£47 10 0.** For **£17 12 6**

$3\frac{1}{4} \times 2\frac{1}{4}$ Dallmeyer Rollfilm, $4\frac{1}{4}$in. Pentac F/2.9 Anastigmat lens, Compur shutter, speeds 1 to 1/150th sec., direct vision view finder, leather case, in good condition. Original price **£17 10 0.** For **£9 12 6**

$4\frac{1}{4} \times 3\frac{1}{4}$ N. & G. New Ideal Sibyl, Ross F/4.5 Xpres lens, 6 single plate-holders, filmpack-holder, leather case, in good condition. List price **£28 10 0.** For **£12 17 6**

$3\frac{1}{2} \times 2\frac{1}{2}$ Sinclair Una, revolving back, double extension, $4\frac{3}{4}$in. Ross F/5.5 Combinable lens, N.S. shutter, 6 double plate-holders, filmpack-holder, set of colour filters, leather case, in good condition. List price **£36.** For **£17 17 6**

$8\frac{1}{2} \times 6\frac{1}{2}$ Adams Studio Minex Reflex, Adams Silent Focal Plane shutter, giving a range of exposures from $\frac{1}{4}$-sec. to 1/64th sec., also Time and Bulb movement, extra long extension, rack rising and swing front, reversing back, 6 best quality double plate-holders, focussing canopy on wire frame, 15in. Cooke Series II A F/45. Portrait Anastigmat lens with soft focus adjustment, Mahogany stand with rising and falling movement, storage box for camera and slides. Cost over **£150.** For half price **£75 0 0**

Price without lens **£55 0 0**

16 mm. Model B Cine Kodak, for 50ft. or 100ft. daylight loading film, Kodak F/3.5 Anastigmat lens, in good condition. Original price **£25** For...... **£9 12 6**

16 mm. Model B Cine Kodak, for 50ft. or 100ft. daylight loading film, Kodak F/1.9 Anastigmat lens, leather case, in excellent condition. List price **£32 10 0.** For **£17 10 0**

15in. Taylor-Hobson Cooke F/5.8 Telephoto, leather case, suitable for postcard or smaller Reflex camera, new condition. List price **£20 10 0.** For **£12 12 0**

12in. Dallmeyer Dallon F/3.5 Telephoto, suitable for 9 × 12 cm. or $\frac{1}{2}$-plate Reflex, lens hood, leather case, in brand new condition. List price **£38.** For **£22 10 0**

11in. Ross F/5.5 Teleros, suitable for $\frac{1}{4}$-plate Reflex, leather case, in excellent condition. List price **£14.** For **£9 7 6**

32-page Catalogue of Second-hand Cameras, Lenses, Enlargers, Cine Cameras and Projectors, Accessories. **£20,000** stock of High-grade apparatus offered at keenly competitive prices. Write for a copy to-day.

SANDS, HUNTER & Co. Ltd.

37 Bedford Street Strand London WC2

Advertisements circa 1933.

to watch a big clock. The developer was about ten minutes, stop bath a couple of minutes and ten minutes for fixing. After the last wash, which took about twenty minutes, the films would be taken out to a huge galvanised iron dryer that looked like a house. It had gas jets in the walls either side to heat it up. The wet films were hung inside at one end and slowly moved through to the other when they would be dry. Sometimes they swung and stuck to each other. They were then put in specially made boxes with a rod sticking up over which the hole in the clip fitted and were taken to the printing room.

The printing room had three printing machines on a platform, each operated by a girl. She had to work out which type of paper to use according to the quality of the negative, whether it had been over or under exposed or perfect (which wasn't very often). They had three boxes of paper, soft, hard or normal. They placed the paper on top of each negative and pressed the foot switch while counting seconds. You only learned through experience what exposure to give it. The exposed paper was passed down a chute from the printing machine to a girl who processed them in a huge dish. She had dozens of prints at a time from the machines that never let up. She had to decide when each one was developed enough and nip it out with her print tongs, like big tweezers, before it went too dark. Sometimes she would be covering two chutes coming at her. The each one was flicked through a stop bath, fixer and wash. To dry the prints and give them a gloss finish we had to squeegee them picture side down onto shiny metal plates and let them dry naturally. We had to keep our fingers crossed that they wouldn't get stuck fast.

Most of the films were from No2 Brownie size or VPK or 1A [typically 2.25 x 3.25 inches (6cm x 8.3cm)] so the negative was quite large and contact prints were big enough to see easily. Our fingernails were always brown from the chemicals. We used to try and scrape it off if we went out to a dance.

Kodak Electric Drum Glazing machine. Wet washed prints are placed picture side up on the left hand canvas belt. This presses them onto the hot chrome drum which is rotating slowly. The prints dry in contact with the drum and fall of onto the cross belt and into a collecting box.

About the third year I was there we were taken over by Kodak and things began to improve. We were sent a big glazing machine, a motor driven heated chrome plated drum with a canvas belt going around it. A girl stood at the end of the machine and put the washed prints face up on the canvass belt which pressed them around the drum. They would fall off into a tray at the front all nicely dried and glazed. Then each print had to be trimmed and sorted by the number on the back and placed in the packet clipped to the film which would also be cut up into individual negatives. Finally it went to the office to be priced and sent back to whichever chemist it had originally come from. These were delivered by three errand boys on butchers bikes. I remember one, Alfie Lecount who was later an officer in the fire service. Also a Dickey Drew. By the fourth season the firm had acquired a car for the out of town deliveries.

We made up all our own developer and fixer from separate chemicals. So much Metol, Sulphite, Carbonate, Bromide, Hypo and Acetic Acid etc. Bleach and Sulphide for Sepia Toner. We had what we called the chemical cupboard which was a room under the platform on which the processing tanks stood.

Standard Metol-Hydroquinone developer

	Grams
Metol	5
Hydroquinone	5
Soda Sulphite crystals	60
Soda Carbonate crystals	60
Potassium Bromide	0.5
Wetting agent	5cc
Water	1000cc

The girls from Stuarts 'Having a good time on the moor' at Yelverton
Left to right:
Elsie Parker, Winnie Bourne, Dorothy Bray, unknown, Ivy Hunwicks, Beaty Harris, Cissy Piper, Hilda Brimacombe, Carrie Caroo and Ivy Vokes.

When we weren't busy we went down there to weigh and packet up the different chemicals ready for use when changing developer or fixer, which had to be done about once a week.

We diluted glacial acetic acid for the stop bath wash. Once I was tipping up the huge acetic acid bottle,

> Glacial acetic acid is the very concentrated form of acetic acid commonly used as a caustic for removing warts and corns. It is a clear liquid with a very pungent odour which freezes at 16.7°C and boils at 118°C. Consequently if stored in a cool room the liquid acid will solidify to an ice like block. This what happened to the contents of Ivy's bottle which had thawed a little around the edge and run up the bottle when it was tipped. Vinegar is 5% dilute acetic acid and photographers have used white distilled vinegar as a stop bath in an emergency.
>
> A 5% acetic acid stop bath is used in photographic processing between the developer and the fixer. The developer is strongly alkali while the fixer (which stabilises the developed image and removes undeveloped emulsion) is acid. When the print or film has been in the developer for the required time it is transferred to the stop bath which arrests the action of the developer immediately and neutralises the alkali in the emulsion so extending the life of the fixer. Developer chemicals oxidise and weaken as they are used and last just one day. Fixer has a much longer life, typically a couple of weeks depending upon throughput. Stuarts were running two fixing tanks. The one following the stop bath would weaken first and be replaced by the next in line. A fresh one was made up and placed last in line.

which had a habit of freezing, to get about 18cc of liquid acid out when the frozen lump inside the bottle slipped forward and changed the balance. I dropped the bottle which smashed. Rather than waste the Acetic Acid I picked up the pieces of acid ice with my bare hands. I didn't feel any pain but the next day I had to go to the casualty department of the hospital as all the skin peeled off my hands like a glove.

Another time we had left the hose running too fast in the wash tanks. They overflowed, there was such a flood which poured down into the chemical cupboard. We were walking about down there with umbrellas up trying to mop it up and save what chemicals we could before Mr Bailey came back. By this time there were three of us working in the film developing room and I was in charge, at the age of 16. I didn't want to face him alone so I said to Mary Allen "I'm coming home to dinner with you!" She lived down Alexander Road, we had an hour and a quarter for lunch. We were so afraid of getting the sack in those days but Jack was a lovely boss really. We had very small wages and long hours but were very happy and glad to have a job. If we were working overtime at the height of the season sometimes we had to hide in the cellar when the factory inspector came around because as teenagers we were only allowed to work certain hours. Even then we used to leave at 8pm. We used to work all hours there during the season and one evening I came out to find my bike gone. I had the number and told the police. They found it three weeks later at Crownhill, painted grey.

We girls used to pay sixpence (2.5p) to take the train up to Yelverton for a day out altogether.

There was a Mrs Dalton who worked there. She did a days work at Stuarts and then went to the Empire Electric cinema in Union Street, where she played the piano to accompany the silent films. However, this was 1930 and the previous year 'The Jazz Singer' was made and talkies had arrived. Not all cinemas were converted for sound so Mrs Dalton had some work yet. [>**Cinemas**]

Stuarts end of season party in Artisan Dwellings 1931.
Ivy Hunwicks front right.

At the end of the season we always had a party. Then I had to find work from September to April when I could go back to Stuart's.

WINTER WORK AND UNEMPLOYMENT

I tried my hand at service in a house at Hartley but finished up with housemaids knee. You were afraid to give up your job because you had to go before the Labour Exchange board to prove that you had good reason. I passed that alright because they examined the knee and said that they always had trouble with people they sent to that house.

If you were out of work in those days you had to go to a school for the unemployed. This was St Levan's Road School, 6miles from where I lived in Hooe. I used to ride my bike there. We learned a bit of typing and shorthand amongst other things, you had to go to school or you would lose your dole. This was 10s 9d (54p) I remember that particularly because one week I arrived home to mum with only the 9d. The ten shilling note had blown away coming across Laira Bridge! You were sent out with a card if any jobs came in and you had to have this card signed by the would-be employer to prove you had gone for it.

Once I was riding home in pouring rain and got the wheel of my bike stuck in the tram lines on Friary Bridge. Once you were in them you knew there was only one way you were going to go. I fell under a horse and cart and was covered in mud. I turned my coat inside out and rode home to Hooe rather shaken.

While I was going to St Levan's School Lady Astor presented me with a small Bible as a prize for General Knowledge. I didn't have much competition. The Bible ended up getting burnt many years later in my husband's lorry when they were ordered to carry out a scorched earth policy while retreating through France to Dunkirk.

The first winter I worked for a while in a raincoat shop but the two winters after that I worked at Crosses in Exeter Street, where the Plaza is now, making up wallpaper books. After that I went to the Defiance Clothing Works on Mill Lane. You worked in fours there on machines. You started on the sleeves of men's suits then went on to pockets but you never learned to make the whole suit. There were long pressing tables up through the centre of the room and every piece was pressed as it was made. What a place that was for bad language! The foreman used to march up and down the whole time cursing and swearing about getting on with the work. I was quite shocked, even with the words on the ladies' toilet walls. The worst time was on a Friday, pay-day. The pay kiosk was halfway down the stairs of this several storied building and everyone seemed to rush to get down those stairs so the foreman would stand at the door to try and slow them up a bit. You could be in the queue for ages. I found out a trick or two after a while, such as if you had one of your work mates further down the stairs she could call you down. It wasn't as if the wage packet was much when you got to the kiosk pigeon hole, somewhere around 11s 2d (56p) a week and as you progressed it went up to 13s 4d (67p). I was glad to get back to Stuarts. In the meantime Kodak had taken them over and at the end of my fourth season I wanted to get something more permanent.

SWIFT STUDIOS

Jeromes Photographers was in Union Street and the boss, Mr Kirby, decided to start a photographer's

Radford House 1931. Swift Studios.

Swift Studios at 37 Frankfort Street 1931. This is now under New George Street.

studio of his own. In 1931 he opened Swift Studios at 37 Frankfort Street, opposite the Western Morning News office. He employed me and the years I spent there were some of the happiest in my life. I had some experience at Stuart's of printing and developing stacks and stacks of postcard views for the shops, all sepia toned. We had a continuous queue of people wanting to be photographed for three prints for 6d (2.5p) or sepia with black background or vignette at three prints for 1s (5p). I loved it there, we were always busy. You could get out on the studio roof and I had my photograph taken up there.

It was a lovely atmosphere on a Saturday night with all the barrow men selling their fruit and the organ grinder playing to people queueing for the Regent Cinema. **[>Cinemas]**

We worked long hours but loved it: 9.30am to 8pm Monday and Tuesday, Wednesday off then 9.30am to 8pm Thursday and Friday, Saturdays 9.30am to 9pm and Sundays 11am to 8pm. We did a lot of print copying work too for people who did not have the negative.

Mr Kirby was a smashing boss and he got on well in competition with Jeromes so he opened up another studio at 182 Union Street, quite near The Posado and another at 13 Sidwell Street, Exeter.

Ivy on the roof of Swift Studios, Frankfort Street.

Swift Studios copy work 1932. Subject unknown.

I was an operator by that time and used to take the photos. The camera produced cardboard negatives in threes. These would be transferred from the camera into a light tight box and taken over to Frankfort Street for processing. There were only two of us in this shop, me taking the photographs and a girl called Betty Shute taking the orders and hand colouring photos while you waited.

When we left work in the evenings we would sometimes go down Union Street or up on the Hoe. You met your friends up there. People just walked up and down in groups. Sometimes we used to go into the amusement arcade to the left of The Palace Theatre where I did see a nasty accident. A sailor, who was drunk, fell off the chairoplane as it was going around. If there was any trouble, which was rare, the provost's van was quickly on the scene.

COURTING AND MARRIAGE

I started courting about this time. A soldier in the Worcestershire Regiment stationed at Crownhill. He was one of twins in the regiment and had lost his brother at Tregantle. Just about every regiment that came there lost a soldier in the very dangerous quicksands there. However because of this tragedy he had started to drink heavily so I had to give him up.

Just when I vowed not to have anything to do with men I met Bill. I was cycling on my own over around Whitsands and I was offered a mug of tea by one of a group of soldiers outside Tregantle Fort cookhouse. It was only an old enamel mug but we stood and talked over it. He made a date to meet me in Plymouth by Derry's Clock the following week. My girlfriend was mad with me because she wanted to go somewhere else but if I made a promise I tried to keep it so I said,

"Look, he won't be there but I'll ride around the clock to say I kept my side of the bargain, then we can go on."

When I got there I didn't recognise him at first in his smart civvies. We ended up going to the pictures. This was July 1935 and we got married in 1936.

Bill and Ivy at Jennycliff, just engaged, 1935.

Ivy aged 21 in 1934 on the end of Hooe Quay. The three boats moored together behind her remained there and rotted away by 2011

Bill Cox on duty outside the main gate of Plumer Barracks, Crownhill, Plymouth. Gentleman on the left unknown.

It was the 6th of July at Hooe St. John's and we couldn't have any photographs taken because it just rained in sheets. We had a one week honeymoon

> Excerpt from the Plymstock Parish Register:
> William Frederick Cox. Age 27. Private in the Suffolk Regiment, son of Edgar Cox, agricultural labourer.
> Married:
> Ivy Irene Hunwicks Age 22. Daughter of Herbert Henry Hunwicks, retd Warrant Officer RN of Beach Cottage, Hooe.

at his home in Dalham, which is six miles from Newmarket. Immediately on coming back to Plymouth he had to go away on manoeuvres. When he came back we had our wedding photos taken by

Bill Cox 1935 Ivy took this photograph of Bill in Swift Studios. "It seems odd now to see someone with a pipe but it was quite usual then."

Above
Bill with his mother and father at Dalham.

Left
Ivy with Bill's father and his bees at Dalham 1936.

my boss at Swift Studios.

We took a room at Crownhill with a Mr and Mrs Hockaday for 10 shillings (50p) a week. We had a stove and a bed. If we wanted a bath we brought it in from the garden and bathed down in their kitchen. It sounds a bit primitive now but we were very happy there. Bill was stationed at Plumer Barracks, Crownhill and I was still working at Swift's. When Bill got off duty he used to come down to Swift Studio. Sometimes he would have to wait ages for me to finish in the evenings so he'd go up to 'The Chocolate Kid', a Saturday market stall at the back of Woolworths, Old Cornwall Street, to buy a box of chocolates. Then he'd come down the lane at the back of Swift's and shout up to me that he'd got some chocolates to, like, tempt me down.

This only lasted six months though. Later in 1936 Bill was posted to Malta and sailed in 1937 on HMT Dunera. **[>HMT Dunera]**

All Marriages are happy. It is the living together after marriage that causes all the trouble.

Bill was an all-in wrestling champion in the army. When he got married his mates sent him this card. On the back is written:
Congratulations from F4 Room. Are you still Champ or has the opposite sex won? Look out for the leg lock.
Ray SF Bogey.

Ivy and Bill's wedding photograph taken in Swift Studios 1936

Left to Right.
Standing Back Row: Jock Cowlrick, B. Wilson (Best Man, later killed in the War), Bill Cox (Bridegroom), Herbert Hunwicks (Ivy's Father).

Sitting, Middle row: Edie Cowlrick (Ivy's best friend), Nellie Hunwicks (Ivy's Sister), Ivy Hunwicks (Bride), Caroline Hunwicks (Ivy's Mother), Ernie Hunwicks (Ivy's Brother).

Sitting on floor: Eddie Hunwicks (Ivy's brother), Betty Hunwicks (Ivy's Sister).

SWIFT STUDIOS
Artist Photographers

182, Union Street, Plymouth.
13, Sidwell Street, Exeter.

Child Portraiture a Speciality
Proprietor: H. W. KIRBY

Wedding Groups and Outdoor Work etc. at short notice

Head Office—37, Frankfort Street.

PLYMOUTH 24 January 1937

To whom it may concern:

Miss I. Hummicks has been in my employ for over five years as Bromide Printer and enlarger. She is also a good Card negative retoucher, Film developer and Printer.

During the whole of her service she has given every satisfaction; being a good quick clean worker, taking pains with her work, to get the best results. She is also quite a good operator.

Always punctual, clean, honest, and trustworthy. I can thoroughly recommend her for any position.

She is leaving us now on her marriage. I wish her every success in the future.

Signed H. W. Kirby

Ivy contributed the following in November 2010.
'Around Hooe Quay in the 1930's'

Walking from the quay to the Royal Oak. First was Mr and Mrs Andrews and [their] son. Their house was on the quay on the left, see photo on bottom of page six. He was a boatbuilder. Still on the left was Mr and Mrs Oxland with two daughters, Joan and Vera and three sons, Arthur, Clifford and Lewis.

Then a three storey house, the Burgoynes, sons Len, Cyril and Stan. Then the alleyway up to the square at the back of the Royal Oak which was run by Mr and Mrs Furse, sons Bill and Frank.

Bill married Ada Hine from the Post Office. Frank was drowned during the war.

On the right hand side of the quay, where the boat slipway and landing stage is now, was a small cottage. Living there at different times: Mrs Rouse, Stanley Edgecombe and May Jolliffe. Still on the righ a long passage with a cottage at the end overlooking the lake. [What is now the garden of Oak Cottage]. People I remember there are Blanche, nee Gale, and her husband Sid Dalton and their daughter Marjorie. They later shifted to America as Marjorie married a GI. She has since visited Hooe St. John's Church.

A Mr and Mrs Tucker then lived there, they shifted to Hexton Hill and ran the paper round before shifting to Turnchapel to run a shop [Tucker's stores, now a private house]. Family Sidney, Alice, Dorothy, Rose, Mervyn, Vi, Megan and Beryl. Sidney and Mervyn were drowned in the war. Alice married a Cole. Dorothy married a soldier who worked at St Anne's house, Jennycliff. Megan married an airman and moved to Australia. Vi married a soldier in the artillery called Robinson. She may still be living in the houses up Jennycliffe Lane. Rose married a Gilbert.

Still on the right from the quay, No2 Beach Cottage occupied by Mr and Mrs Gale. He was a soldier at Brownhill Battery, Bovisand. Their daughters Blanche, Lovey, Alice and Emily. Sons: Arthur, Jack, Walter and Harold. Blanche went to America, Lovey, Alice and Emily moved to London. Arthur worked on the roads, Jack joined the Navy, Walter worked at Warrens Garage [Dean's Cross] and was later manager of the Cement Works at Billacombe. He had a beautiful voice and married Mr Badge's daughter. Badge was the local policeman who lived in Turnchapel. Harold lived on Hexton Hill.

I lived in No1 Beach Cottage. Mum and Dad Hunwicks and daughters Ivy, Nellie and Betty. Sons: Ernie and Eddie. Dad was in the Navy. When he came out in the 1930's he was many other things. Door to door salesman, window cleaner, Chimney sweep, drain cleaner at Mount Batten, Barber for the village children, shoe repairer, Devon County referee, Chairman of Hooe St. John's football team, on different committees and general scribe for the village. He was called back into the Navy and was signal boatswain in charge of the signal station at St. Margaret's Bay, Dover. He died age 64.

Mothers never worked outside the house. All of these two families used the one toilet in the front court, next to the wash house. The houses consisted of a front room and a living room and two bedrooms. The front room overlooked the lake. Dad's piano took up most of it. The living room was table and chairs, food cupboard, gas stove, and a small recess with curtains across where we washed and kept a couple of buckets in case one of us was caught short. A zinc bath was hung on the wall outside. A tap in the corner and two clothes lines. We gathered wood from Hooe Brakes for the four open fires and the copper.

Next door [Oak Cottage] was old Mrs Dolton and sons Harold, Syd and Len. Daughter Francis. There was a much shorter wall between No1 and the Doltons, we were able to talk over it. After the Doltons left a family called Henley lived there.

Hooe c1900 before the building of Beach Cottage

CHAPTER 3
Malta and War

I still kept my work on and saved to get the £9 for the fare to join him. I was taking a lot of passport photos so was always asking where people were going. I got friendly with a sailor's wife, Edna Higgins, her family came from Turnchapel, because she was saving to go to Malta too. On 4th June 1938 we travelled out together on the SS Moreton Bay.

Built by Vickers Ltd, Barrow, in 1921 for the Australian Commonwealth Line the Moreton Bay was 13,855 gross tons, length 530.6ft x beam 68.3ft (161,73m x 20,81m), one funnel, two masts, twin screw and a speed of 15 knots.

Her regular route was Southampton, Malta, Port Said, Colombo, Freemantle, Adelaide, Sydney and Brisbane with, in 1938, room for 542 single class passengers.

In 1939 she was commissioned as an Armed Merchant Cruiser and in 1941 she was converted into a troopship. In 1946 she reverted to commercial service between London, Colombo, and Sydney. Her final sailing was on 30th Nov1956 and on 13th Apr1957 she arrived at Barrow for scrapping.

Edna Higgins (left) and Ivy on the SS Moreton Bay en-route to Malta in 1938.

Bill met me at the dock. He had come in a taxi which was an old American Plymouth, would you believe. He rushed towards me but I shouted,

"Don't touch me!"

You see I was, well Edna and I both, were very badly sunburned. Not realising the difference between the sun in England and the Mediterranean sun, which was much stronger, we had just lain on deck enjoying it.

He had managed to get us a first floor flat near Dragonara Palace about a mile and a half from his barracks, which were at St. George's Bay.

Bill on the veranda of the flat in Dragonara Palace.

We had a large front room, a bedroom, kitchen and upstairs room for the maid. There was everything there for us, down to knives and forks for 10s (50p) a week. Mind you Bill only got 30s (£1.50) a week as an unpaid Lance Corporal but we did get rations.

Front room of married quarters in St George's Bay. Winter 1938.

There was a big joint of meat twice a week and bread too because Bill was 26 so he was what was called 'on the strength'. Once a month we were issued with so much for 'condiments' about 1s/6d (7.5p). We never wanted a maid as we had no children. The other couple in the bottom flat had one so we changed flats with them so they could have a baby sitter. It was really beautiful there. The only trouble we had was when the army issue came with the blocks of ice for our ice box. We would put a bowl out for it and the Maltese would pinch it on their way home from the small church on top of the hill. That, or mats or anything really that was left outside in the early morning.

We were still waiting for a proper married quarter; luckily we were able to swap our flat for a married quarter occupied by Bandsman and Mrs Jenner. She couldn't get on with her neighbours so we swapped over to St Georges' Bay into what they called 'The Bird Cage.'

There were about twelve quarters there and we had one on top in the centre. We could run down to the sea. Cockroaches were the problem there. They'd be all along the mantelpiece, under the table and in the little kitchen. We'd get the table out onto the veranda every so often. We had a Flit (insecticide) issue and we'd spray them out into the open and then hit them with our slippers.

> Flit was a popular insecticide supplied in rectangular tins and applied with a hand sprayer that soon gave its name to all similar sprayers. The Flit Gun was user fillable so could be used to spray any other liquids and has been used in applications as diverse as custom car painting and ceramic glaze application.
>
> Flit insecticide was Paraffin with Pyrethrum added. Later DDT was used (invented in 1939). As Ivy mentions it was not totally effective against cockroaches but worried them enough to drive them out into the open where they could be whacked. It was more effective against flies and mosquitos.
>
> 'My mother has a flit gun,
> It's not devoid of charm.
> A bit of Flit shot out of it,
> The rest shot up her arm!'
>
> Pam Ayres

St Georges' Bay, Malta 1938.
Ivy and Bill's quarters were in the front building, by the waterside, in the centre of the upper verandha. These quarters were nicknamed 'The Bird Cage'. The building behind was St Georges' Barracks.

But war was looming. The soldiers started to dig trenches and our quarters were gas proofed so that in the event of a gas attack the families would bring the children up there. The Devon Regiment were in St Andrews' barracks and we were with the

Suffolks' in St Georges' Bay. It was a toss-up who would be sent home first to get ready for France. We made our own entertainment, I seem to remember that playing Bingo for matches was very popular.

Bingo for matches on the terrace of The Bird Cage.

Altar in the small church near Dragonara.

TO PLYMOUTH AND THE WAR

We were sent home in the June of 1939 on HMT Lancashire and war broke out in September. They lost a lot of the Devon Regiment families when they finally left. I was very sea sick on our journey home as I was two months pregnant with our first baby.

We came back to Granby Barracks, Devonport on a very damp drizzly day. Our issue of bedding was just dumped on the square and we took over a condemned quarter. It was filthy, with remains of food still in the oven from the previous tenant. Also mice had taken over. We set to, dried our bedding out, cleaned it up and settled in best we could.

They were just finishing off some new quarters, up at the back along by Devonport Park and we got a good brand new home and were very happy to move into it. Our happiness didn't last long though because the men were moved to Axminster, so we women went up there to be with our men as long as we could before they had to go to war. They were told that they would be there a week but after two days we had to come back to Plymouth because they were on the move again.

The men went to Axbridge so a friend took me up there in a little baby Austin car a couple of times. Then the men were on the move again, they never knew where they were going. This time they came back to Plymouth and ended up somewhere along the Embankment. People from the council houses there went down with eats and cups of tea for them. My husband came home to me and said he thought they would be there for a week, but it didn't turn out like that.

I felt fine that day, I had just finished knitting a pram cover and been down to Fore Street to buy some fish for tea, which was Bill's favourite. I sat down waiting for him to come home when a post office messenger came to the door with a message: 'Sorry Darling. Can't get home. Leaving Dukes' Dock for France.'

'The Birdcage' and St George's Bay Hotels, Malta 2000.

HMT Lancashire, aboard which Ivy and Bill returned to Plymouth. Built 1914. Converted to troopship 1930. Scrapped 1956. 9542 tons.

I just didn't know what to do so I got a scuttle of coal in and lit the fire. The lifting of the coal scuttle and the shock and all started me losing the baby. All I could do was go to bed and put my legs up on a chair and try to stop it. We had arranged for my sister to come out and stay with me but she didn't leave work until 8 o'clock. I ended up in the military hospital by Stonehouse Bridge.

There was chaos there with nurses and Red Cross volunteers and they let us know that they hadn't joined up to look after soldiers' wives. There were two wives out of the regiment who had pleurisy. I laid in there for a fortnight hoping to keep the baby then I was given an enema by one of the VAP's, which she should not have done I found out afterwards. I could feel the baby coming, there was no-one in the ward but other patients and no bell by the bed. I started to throw books and anything down the middle of the ward to attract attention.
When the Matron and a Nurse finally arrived the baby had been born. They put it up on a pillow so I could see it. It looked quite alright, then they took it away and I heard it crying for half an hour, then they came in to tell me that it had died.

I stayed in there six weeks waiting for a doctor as I was still bleeding and they hadn't got the operating theatre ready. I thought Bill was in France but he told me afterwards that at the time he was still on a ship in Plymouth Sound and could have got compassionate leave had he known. The regimental major's wife came in and saw that the baby was christened and buried somewhere in a Plymouth cemetery.

When I got better I gave up the married quarter and went back to live with mum at Hooe. Then I felt that I needed to get away for a while so I went up to Suffolk to stay with Bill's mum for a couple of months. I always had the photographic journal and I was reading through the adverts one day and saw that Swift Studios were advertising for staff so I came back to Plymouth and my old job. It didn't last long though because by May 1940 we had Dunkirk. We saw train loads of wounded coming in on the train at Turnchapel.

I was frantic with worry because on the news they kept saying everyone is out now and I still hadn't heard from Bill. Then I received a post card and written in pencil was 'Arrived safe this morning. Will write later. All my love, Bill.' The WRVS women were taking the cards and posting them for the soldiers.

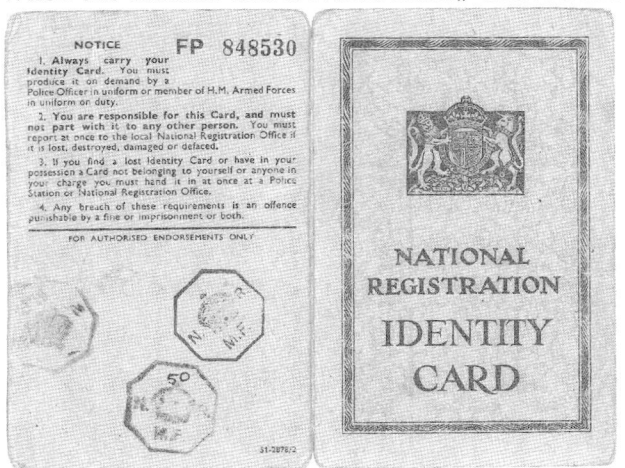

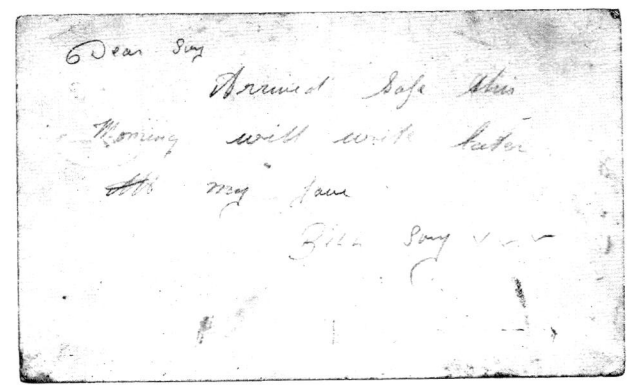

Then one day I came home from work and people in the village said "Your husband's home!" He was in rags. His trousers were all ripped up and he was tied up with string. He had shrapnel in his legs, well, he had been in the rearguard and standing in and out of water for five days before getting a boat home. It was quite a small boat and they were being shelled and fired at on the way across the channel.

When he reported back for duty he ended up in a mushroom farm at Cucklington in Somerset. People were wonderful in that village and they offered rooms so us wives could go up. The lady I went up to was a farmers' daughter at Chilthorne Domer, just north of Yeovil and we have been like sisters ever since.

Later in 1940 I was back in Plymouth and we were getting very severe air raids. I was still working at Swift Studios and one of our girls had a birthday party in the Laira narrows. I went to it and during the party there was all hell let loose. Bombs dropping everywhere. We could look across the Plym to the Laira Bridge, it was the old iron bridge then, which looked all on fire along with the bus station so I couldn't cross the bridge to get home. We all dossed down on her floor. Another time I got as far as Plymstock and it got so bad I stopped at a friends house at Randwick.

My sister Nellie had a three month old baby, Joan, so together we decided to take a flat in 7 Fanshawe Terrace, Hooe. We moved in on the Wednesday and were bombed out the following Monday. We had gone round the sale rooms and bought some furniture but we didn't even have time to get the place straight. That Monday my sister was staying in the flat and I was visiting friends in Plymstock. My mother had walked up to Plymstock to tell me not to be frightened when I returned to the flat as a bomb had dropped in the garden knocking the front

Bill and Ivy 1940. After Dunkirk.

7 Fanshawe Terrace after the bomb that fell in the front garden.

out but that my sister and her baby were OK. We used to get under the stairs in these raids and if I had been home that night the huge pieces of bomb which went through the gas cupboard wall and into the bedroom could have killed me. As it was they missed Nellie and Joan but they were covered in plaster dust.

What a sight greeted me when we got home. In our bedroom we had an iron bedstead and the shrapnel from the bomb had cut right through it. The glass from the wardrobe was smashed over the bed and all the clothes in the wardrobe had shrapnel holes all around the bottoms to about six inches (153mm) up. I shortened the coats afterwards and still wore them.

What happened then was that Edie and Jock Cowlrick at Randwick took us in. Our furniture was stacked at the back of Fanshawe, waiting for the council to come and see if we would get any compensation. I think it worked out to about 23 shillings (£1.15) Because we needed a bed at Edie's, there were already four in their family, we got a friend to go down with his lorry to bring up a bed settee which we had bought second hand in Ebrington Street. We hadn't had a chance to inspect it before we got down to a good nights sleep, as we thought. Suddenly Nell wakes me up and says "Whatever's that in the bed?". It was full of bed bugs and the worst of it was we were in someone else's house with this lot. We had to get the whole house fumigated and we couldn't get rid of the bed quick enough. I went into the shop where we bought it and said "As we were bombed out would he care to buy it back cheaper?" I never mentioned the bugs!

Ivy in her shortened coat.

During the war a full length warm coat was difficult to get, due to rationing and shortages. A solution was to make one yourself from a bed blanket.
Like this one of Ivy's.

Mum was still down in No 1 Beach Cottage overlooking Hooe Lake. She had my young sister and two brothers still there and when the oil tanks across the

7 Fanshawe Terrace 2002.

lake at Turnchapel caught fire all the smoke and oil came over the lake and into the village. All the food was covered in black sooty oily film and there were bombs dropping in the lake all the while they were burning.

We had to get them out of it so we all ended up at my friends. We slept about eight in a bed, four at the top, four at the bottom. My friends mum and dad lived further down the road and they had a shelter in the garden. We spent night after night in there, all squeezed in. It really belonged to a man and his wife who lived in a top flat over my friends parents but this man would not get in the shelter. I

Two surprisingly well turned out boys survey the damage to Hooe village and the burning oil tanks.   Western Morning News.

remember one night I must have dozed off to sleep and woke up suddenly to see this shape holding his pipe in the entrance to the shelter and I thought it was Hitler arrived.

In the meantime we were trying to get to work but never knew if our shop would still be there. We were right opposite the Western Morning News office and I can remember one morning going in to work and Costers was all on fire. We had to get over and under fire hoses and some ways were blocked off because of unexploded bombs. We finally reached Swifts by going down through the Regent /Odeon Cinema and up a back lane. Incidentally Hitler did a bit of good there as the barrow boys had all their stores up that lane and there were plenty of rats about. One morning I found two in the bowl of the outside toilet and once I remember Mr Kirby, our boss, got a gun and said to us girls "You stop after work and we'll have a bit of fun with these rats." We stood on the steps with our heads level with the floor of the room above and he shot them as they appeared.

Eventually we lost both our shops and I decided to try and follow Bill as he was moving around England after Dunkirk. For one thing I had lost one child and we both wanted children. I thought it could be years if he was posted abroad again. He was moved from Cucklington to Weymouth, he was in the school up on the hill, and at 36 had his tonsils out in Portland Hospital so I went up and lodged with a Mrs Chalker at Wyke Regis. Her husband was an air raid warden and she was a WRVS on a canteen van. We had the ack-ack [anti-aircraft] guns just across the road. As soon as an enemy plane was spotted off went this lot and the Germans were firing back with machine guns, I had been left alone in the house and had to keep getting under the bed. I stuck it for one night and then asked Mrs Chalker if I could come out with her in the canteen van because I would rather be doing something. Wherever a bomb dropped they had to go so we were going to the shelters handing out cups of tea and keeping the firemen supplied with sandwiches. I quite enjoyed that as you felt no fear if you were kept busy.

This was during the Battle of Britain and as I walked backwards and forwards to the hospital to see Bill I used to look up and planes were fighting so high they looked like flies. Then Bill got posted to Swanage and I moved into a room there in a house near the end of the railway line. In the meantime my friends, Edie and Jock Cowlrick, decided to leave Plymouth and went to live at Heath and Reach, just north of Leighton Buzzard, where Jock, her husband, had been born.

One strange experience we had while at Swanage was that we went for a walk along the Purbeck Hills and there was a little chuchyard up there. A woman was kneeling at the grave of a German airman and she asked us if we would say a prayer for him.

I don't know what we said but after all we had been through we didn't go much on the idea. But we had a shock because she then took us to her airman son's grave; it was a case of one mother thinking about another across the sea. We often thought about that.

Bill and I were still coming back to Plymouth when he had leave and my mother and the rest of the family had managed to rent a house in Manor Road,

Swift Studios bombed in 1940/41. View West along Frankfort Street towards the Regent/Odeon.

Pomphlett. Number 29 it was. You could actually buy these houses very cheaply, around £750 I think, as everyone wanted to leave Plymouth.

29 Manor Road, Pomphlett, with Australian airmen circa 1943.

29 Manor Road, Pomphlett 2003. The dividing wall between the adjoining drives of 29 and 31 has been removed as has the gate and part of the front wall to facilitate car access.

By that time my dad had been called back to the Navy and was a com.sig.boatswain in charge of the signal station at St Margaret's Bay near Margate. One of my brothers was a despatch rider and got injured when the Naval Barracks was hit, my other brother was over in Fishguard. My brother-in-law was an aircraft navigator. I remember one night most of them happened to be on leave at the same time so we walked to the Morley Arms for a drink. While we were there the bombs started to fall all around us and we were knocked to the floor. When we came out we saw that the garage next door had been hit. Before we had our own shelter built in the garden we used to go down to Stamps Corner and use the shelter under the road. We hardly had time to get home from work before it would start. One night I was running down Pomphlett Road past the Blue Peter pub and having to shelter by dropping down into the gutter and losing my shoe.

We were not at Swanage long before Bill was posted to Welwyn Garden City. I had all my papers to go into the WAAF but I never went in because I was overjoyed to discover I was pregnant again! It happened just right because they wouldn't allow camp followers at Welwyn, you had to have a work permit. As I had lost my first baby I decided to go to Edie Cowlrick at Heath and Reach to have the next. It was all quiet there, no bombs. Jock had got work with the London Brick Company, they had a nice flat and there was even a midwife lodging downstairs. Our daughter arrived as the Doctor was doing his rounds and I had the midwife to take care of me. We called the baby Carole. This was July 1942 and Bill came out on leave and took us back to Plymouth.

The war wasn't all doom and gloom because we all lived happily at 29 Manor Road. We had the Americans here by that time and the Australian airmen at Mount Batten. [>**RAAF**] My brother was working with some Americans so he used to bring them home often, or we would meet some Australians down at the Blue Peter and take them home to supper. We had to make the best of things and we never knew when the sirens would go off. We used to play Nap quite late as we were afraid to go to bed. [>**Nap**]

We had some nice times down at the Blue Peter and one New Year's Eve we went to a dance at Mount Batten. The Americans took us out to a place opposite the old Morgue between Hooe and Turnchapel and gave us a party. Plenty of peanut butter I can remember and doughnuts. There were a lot of black Americans at a camp in Dunstone Woods. If you met them around Plymstock they were always polite. One of the Australians had been an opera singer and we used to love to hear him sing

Blue Peter Inn 2003.

but it wasn't like having our own men home. We just whiled away the time hoping that it would soon be over.

My sister's husband was a bomb aimer out in Burma and had to bale out when his plane was hit. He was in the water and reported missing for some time until he was rescued. Preparations were now in hand for the D-Day landings in Normandy and Bill was sent to Scotland on an assault course in preparation. However events took another funny turn and Normandy didn't happen for him. At this time they were also sending troops to Tunis in North Africa and one of the soldiers had jumped ship so Bill was sent in his place. Our daughter was just three months old when he left. She would be over three years old when he saw her again.

My brother got married to Brenda Puleston, a little Welsh girl who went into the WAAF in the tailors shop because she had worked in Berkertex in Plymouth. They hadn't been married long when she discovered she was expecting a baby so she came out of the WAAF. Mr Gill, who had been a reporter for the Western Evening Herald, was advertising for someone to print passport photos part-time in the mornings. He had a little processing and printing set-up in the basement of one of the houses in The Crescent. So I went to work for him and Brenda looked after my little girl.

Mr Gill would go out to the Naval and Marine barracks and take the photographs then bring the camera back, a 35mm Leica it was. I would take the film out, process and print it then take the photos back out to the barracks by No 7 or 14 tram. It was quite easy, there were always plenty of trams around Derry's Clock. Photographic paper was like gold dust and I would have to walk around town getting a box here and there from different chemists. The man who supplied us with most was Mr Crook, the optician. Their shop was in Torrington Place, off Tavistock

Leica advertisement 1934.

Road. He, or his son, later moved down to Frankfort Gate and I still kept in touch with their receptionist who was with them all that time. I was left alone there in the basement of The Crescent developing the film and printing then one day a man called at the door. He wanted to sell Mr Gill a camera. I told him he wasn't there at the moment and I sort of got interested in this camera and thought 'well I could buy that' so I bought it. It was a Russian FED, 35mm and a copy of the Leica. Lovely little camera it was too. That's what I took all my photographs with in the parks. Just going up to people asking if they would like their photograph taken and then people would get to know me.

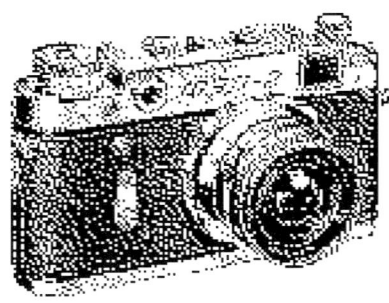

FED 2 35mm Camera.

I had quite a little business going taking people's photos.

We were still getting terrible air raids but by this time we had our own garden shelter. There had been a lull in the bombing so we started going to bed in the house. Then one morning, about 2am, it started again. I wrapped the baby up in a blanket and ran to the shelter at the bottom of the garden. I had to put a spurt on because not only were the Germans bombing us but we used to get a lot of shrapnel from our own anti aircraft guns which were mounted on Colesdown Hill.

Half way down I tripped on the blanket, fell and hit my little daughters head on the stone flower border. I had to wait for my brother to come down to the shelter with his torch on to be able to see what I had done. She was eighteen months old then and had a nasty gash right down across her eyebrow. Living next door at the time was a nurse and she came and bathed it with Dettol and we wrapped her up and took her to the bottom of the road where a policeman directed us to the first aid post which was at Plymstock Secondary school. There was a Doctor Scott there. He put three large stitches in it to stop the bleeding then the bombing started again and we all had to run to the shelter under the school, consequently it was never done properly. When we got home we saw that the bungalow next door to us had been flattened by a direct hit and the people killed. [>**First Aid**]

Shortly afterwards we noticed that Carole was losing weight, not eating properly, was generally very off colour and her head was swelling. I sat up with her for a week as her eyes were shut and swollen not knowing if her eyes were alright. I was told to bathe the wound with warm salt water but as nothing seemed to make any difference I felt that I needed a second opinion so I went to a chemist on Mutley Plain and showed him the baby's head. He said "Go to Greenbank Hospital at once!"

They examined her and said she had pus and poison in her ears because of infection in the wound which they opened and kept open to drain it. She gradually picked up and got better and the wound healed, though she had a nasty scar there for a while. When she was seven she went to Sheffield Children's Hospital where they reopened it and put in a lot of smaller, neater stitches. Some years after the war she was awarded £600 for injuries sustained during the war.

Transcript of a letter from Bill to Ivy, 9th May 1943

Cpl Cox W
'B' Coy 12pl
1st Bnn East Surrey Reg
BNAF

Sunday 9-5

Here I am once again trusting this will find you and all in the best of health as I am O.K. Well, my love, I guess you have heard the good news about the fall of Tunis. It fell into our hands Friday night and we had the honour of marching through on Saturday morning, out the other side to where we are now, Tunis harbour, Lar Goelette, you can see it on the map I think. We had a wonderful reception, they gave us wine, Cigs and Cigars but they told us they had very little food and very little of anything, the Germans and Italians had it all. We told them it would be different now and they nearly went mad. When they saw us poor people but in a few days time it will be all over. We couldn't hardly get up the street, they crowded around us, kissed and shook hands it was really a lovely sight. The blighters wouldn't make a Dunkirk of it, they just gave themselves up left and right. We all feel very happy out here and I guess you all do at home. Keep smiling and we hope this lot will soon be over and we can get back together again. We are in billets again so its not too bad, there is a lot I could say but just can't. Will tell you one day.

Well my love, how is my dear little Carole? I'll bet she is getting on lovely. I haven't had a letter yet but won't be long now, we are all settled down for a time, we hope. Give my love to all at home please. I shall be writing to my mum after this, telling her all the news.

I have got a lovely big cigar on at the moment and feel like Churchill, ha ha. Some of our lads had a terrible experience, they were captured a fortnight ago but they couldn't get them away. The Germans had them on a boat but our air force stopped them and gave them hell, not knowing there were prisoners on board. Anyhow all the Germans and Italians got off and left our lads to get on the best they could. Anyhow they are all with us again now thank God.

I expect you at home know more than we do what's going on, we only know what we see where we are. Well my love I still love you with all my heart and soul and body and always will. Please give my dear little Carole a lovely big kiss please. I can picture her crawling all over the house these days, bless her.

Well my love I will ring off for this time so all my love to my Dear and Darling Sweetheart Wife Ivy and my Dear Baby Carole.

God Bless you all, Bill

During this time Bill was in Africa with the 8th and 1st Army and was transferred to the East Surreys for the big push into Sicily. One of his battalion stepped on a mine and nine soldiers were killed. Bill was blown over a wall and landed in a field.

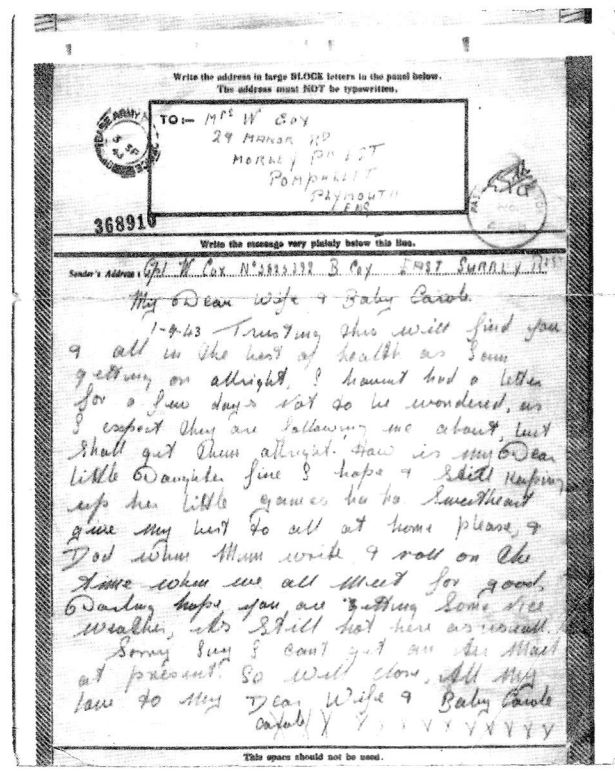

Letter to Ivy from Bill 1st September 1943.

In hospital with his injuries he was graded B6 and transferred, after the battles for Italy, to the Somerset Light Infantry. He went into the prison service in Italy until 1945 when he came home for nineteen days leave and left me expecting my second daughter. I found a poem in his pocket that he must have copied from somewhere when he was out there. He was no poet but it was important to him. I often wonder what the original was, it might have been a song.

Blood on the Sands of Tunisia

There is blood on the sands of Tunisia
'Tis the blood of the brave and the true,
Of three nations together in battle
'Neath the banners of Red White and Blue.

Now as they went o'er the sands of Tunisia,
To the place where the enemy lay,
They remembered the Generals' order
That this pass must be taken today.

Some thought of their wives and their Mothers,
Some thought of their Sweethearts so fair
And some, as they plodded and stumbled,
Were softly whisp'ring a prayer.

So they marched o'er the sands of Tunisia
With faces unsmiling and stern
For they knew as they charged up the hillside
That many would never return.

There is blood on the sands of Tunisia,
'Tis the gift for the freedom they love.
May their names live in glory forever
And their souls rest in Heaven above.

This poem had been published in the North Africa edition of 'Stars and Stripes', the US Military Newspaper, in 1943.
Bill might have seen it there.

Services Air Mail Christmas Card from Tunis.

Hand made Christmas Card from Italy 1943.

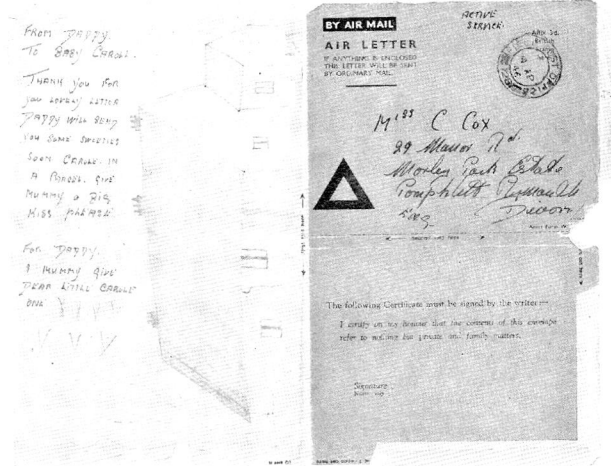

AIR MAIL. 1945
In 1945 Bill was guarding Italian prisoners of war in Italy. One of the prisoners had a flair for cartooning so Bill asked him to draw this cartoon of two RAF(?) officers to which Bill added the caption:

The Two Types by ?
"Yes, I know its a full box old man but only one in each box ever strikes and I was lucky first time."

On the reverse a letter to Carole
From Daddy To Baby Carole.
Thank you for your lovely letter. Daddy will send you some sweeties soon Carole. Give Mummy a BIG kiss please for Daddy. & Mummy give dear little Carole one. XXXXXX

He went back to Italy working in the prisons as they were dealing with war crimes trials by that time and he was in the regular army.

My sister's husband, the bomb aimer, had been rescued from the sea and was coming home from Bangkok. She had a second daughter in July as I had mine in September. Brenda, my sister-in-law looked after her little boy for a while and she looked after ours as well, with mum's help.

I was still working half a day at Gills and my sister went into the Western Morning News office part-time, but it began to get a bit much all in one house.

The flat at 7 Fanshawe Terrace had been done up again by now so we moved back there until our husbands came home. We only had one bedroom there so that got a bit crowded too with our bed and cots for four children.

Then in September 1945 the war came to an end.

To celebrate the end of the war we had a little party on the front lawn of 7 Fanshawe. Suddenly there was a loud bang from across the road. We all jumped and the little ones were crying and saying that their legs hurt.

What had happened was a man in Colonel Coates' field opposite was shooting rabbits with a 12 bore shotgun and some lead shot had come across the road into the children. They did have a few pellet wounds in their legs but no real harm was done. I shall never forget the look on the man's face when he realised what he had done and came to the door as white as a sheet.

*Outside 29 Manor Road, Pomphlett 1945.
Ivy with, L to R, Jean Waldron, Joan (sister Nell's daughter) and Ivy's daughter Carole.*

CHAPTER 4
Post war years

Front of Married Quarters 40 at Williams Road, Chilwell, Nottingham 1947.

I had my second daughter, Maureen, in 1946 in the Alexandra Nursing Home, Devonport. No problems with this one.

Bill came home in 1947 for good and was posted to Nottingham as a caterer for the officers mess. We soon followed him and went into married quarters at Chilwell, between Nottingham centre and Beeston. We had a job to get things right there for a while as the old black range wouldn't work. We had to buy a gas stove ourselves eventually but the next door neighbour, who was in the police, made sure we had a cup of tea after our journey up from Plymouth.

We loved it up there as these quarters were in an orchard right up on a hill. The only trouble was the fog. We used to get real pea soupers. There was one when we arrived and we had been there about a fortnight before it cleared and we could see what was down below us.

We had one fright while we were there. The little boy next door, aged three, Mrs Burrow's son, used to play with my two year old daughter, Maureen. They were always in and out of both houses. Then one morning while we two women were doing our washing and hanging it out I thought my girl was in their house and she thought her boy was in ours but they were nowhere to be seen. Panic struck us, we searched everywhere and consoled ourselves by saying they were only small and couldn't have got far and they couldn't have got out of the main gate as there were always two or three police on there.

Mrs Burrow's husband was home at the time and he grabbed a bike belonging to an insurance man who was doing his rounds as a lady had come in saying she had seen two little ones at the bus stop. So I went to the police station and phoned the bus depot. While Mr Burrows went in one direction towards Longeaton I went in the other towards Beeston. Then after going about ten yards I saw Mr Burrows coming through the fog with the two of them. He had got a little way up the main road and a woman had them by the hand.

She said "The little boy was on the pavement but the little girl was on the island in the middle of the road." It just shows how easy it is to lose children.

Bill was very happy in his job as food was still rationed but there seemed to be plenty in the officers mess. He used to keep rabbits at the back of our house and feed them leftovers from the mess then sell them back to them for meals. It only lasted two years though and in 1949 he was posted back to the Somerset Depot at Taunton. Dad died the same year.

Bill went ahead of us as usual and as there wasn't a quarter available at Taunton at the time we were told that if we took a quarter at Topsham, near Exeter, it would be a stepping stone to one at Taunton barracks. So we came down to Topsham.

There were a group of quarters out in the middle of waist high grass. Bill had been in and got it ready with bedding and so on. It seems they had been used by Americans but had been left empty for some time. Bill had the weekend off to help get us settled in but

that night was a real nightmare for me. I could hear scratch scratching and couldn't sleep because of it. I got up and put the light on "Bill," I says "There's mice or something in here." There was a built in wardrobe opposite the bed and you could see them running in and out under the door.

If there is anything I am terrified of its mice! Bill then told me that he had slept one night here before we came and as he turned the bed sheets back he could see that they had even been in the bed!

Anyway, he went back to Taunton and we had to stick it out in this place in order to get quarters in Taunton. The mice were not the only occupants. I went into the chemist in Topsham and asked if he had anything to get rid of rats, mice, fleas and bugs. We had the lot!

When I went to the cookhouse they said I could borrow their cat so I took it home and went to sleep happy with the thought that the cat would deal with the mice. However because it was locked up in a strange place it ignored the mice and messed everywhere. I don't know what was worse, the cat or the mice.

I asked my mum to come up from Plymouth and we set traps everywhere. When we started to go up to bed there was a snap from the bathroom, a snap from the bedroom, a snap from another trap..

After about three weeks we had the good news that we had quarters allocated to us in Taunton Barracks. The Major showed us into the downstairs flat and said "It's not much I'm afraid, the people who were here before kept coal in the bath but there is a hip bath hanging on the wall outside." I said it was a palace compared to where I had come from. The only trauma we had there was a water shortage and they kept turning it off. One morning about seven am we heard the quartermaster shouting outside so we got up and put our feet into several inches of water. He had noticed it running out under the front door. It turned out that one of my girls had turned a tap on over the little sink the night before, when the water had been turned off at the main, and getting no water hadn't turned it off again.

Maureen's Ration Book at Taunton

We weren't in these quarters long when we got a better upstairs flat where we were very happy. Bill was caterer for the Sergeants Mess and when my youngest daughter was five I went to work for Marks and Spencer, which was just down the road. I started in the canteen then, down on the ice cream counter, then I was in charge of the biscuit counter. We had to save money for Bill was coming out of the Army. He was getting troubled with arthritis now and he had done twenty-two years so he would get a pension.

Suddenly they post him to Aldershot, promote him to Sergeant Major and ask him to stay on. I put my foot down and said that twenty-two years was long enough and our eldest girl, Carole, had already changed school eight times. So he didn't sign on and finished his time as Sergeant Major at Plasterdown Camp near Walkhampton on Dartmoor. He left the Army in 1953. He had always said that when he came out of the Army he would like to be a bus conductor so he got a job with the Western National.

He used to come up some weekends to see us. Once he came up strapped in adhesive plaster because he had broken three ribs. The bus had been going along Ebrington Street when a child ran out into the road.

The driver slammed on the brakes just as Bill was rolling a ticket off one of those machines they used to carry around their neck. He went flying down to the front of the bus and landed on the machine. It turned out he was allergic to the adhesive on the plaster and had huge blisters come up under it. He came back to Plymouth and they took it off and bandaged it instead.

Bill was living at Mum's house in Manor Road, Pomphlett and we had notice to leave the married quarters in Taunton. Being in the services all those years we had no other home. They were building new houses in Plympton at St Maurice estate so I went to the housing office to ask if we could be rehoused there. The housing officer said that they were only for their own local people. I said I was their local people as I was bombed out of Hooe during the war. It still didn't carry any clout. The MoD took us to court in Taunton to get us out of the married quarters. It was quite easy, though I had been dreading it, and they made an order to Plympton council to rehouse us in six weeks.

Bill didn't stay with the Western National long and got a job in the recruiting office at Devonport. I worked one Christmas at Marks and Spencer in Plymouth then I saw an advert in the paper that Kodak, under the name of Stuart Photo Services, were wanting staff in their processing lab at Alvington Road, Cattedown. This had been built on a bomb site soon after the war.

In 1954 I went back to work at Stuarts, which had been taken over by Kodak and moved to Alvington Road, Cattedown.

Stuart's Staff circa 1955, at the Elfordleigh Hotel. One of the annual Dinner Dances.
Front Row. L to R:
George, Sylvia Nicholson (office girl), David, Yvonne Rocky (glazer), Ivy Cox, Kath Heppel, Judy, Pearl Wilkins.
Back Row. L to R:
George (Driver), Margaret Harley, Michael Harley, Ann Morton, Mr Pomeroy (Manager), Marjorie Ryder, Mr Jack Bayley (Director), Dorothy Duke, Muriel Hooper (cleaner).

Stuarts Photo Services building in Alvington Street. 2002.
The increase of small, rapid process in-shop developing and printing machines that could be run by one or two operators meant the end of large centralised D&P labs. The lab was taken over by Marco Marine.

Stuarts staff, 1957.
Front row, L to R: Pat Deacon, Christine, Mike Harley (became manager when Mr Pomeroy left), Martin Wills (Production Manager), Anne Morton, Pearl Wilkins.

Back Row, L to R: Kath Heppel, ?, Georgina Kelland, Yvonne Rocky, Dorothy Duke, Ivy Cox (wearing a blonde wig), Merilyn Lydon, George, ?, ?, Pam, David, Margaret Harley, June Lake.

When I first went back they were still on the old deep tanks system but gradually automation came in with fully automatic colour processing machines so it was a whole new ball game. It certainly took the hard work out of it. We had Mr Pomeroy as manager who I had worked with at the old Notte Street factory where he used to do the enlarging. He had gone into the Air Force during the War.

Stuarts end of season party
Seated Front, L to R: Sylvia Nicholson, Margaret Harley, Ivy Cox.
Standing, L to R: Dorothy Duke, June Lake, ?(driver), Ann Moreton, Mr Pomeroy, Marjorie Ryder, David, ?, Yvonne Rocky.

Stuarts still employed a lot of seasonal workers. In the summer they employed more processing staff and three drivers instead of the usual one.

Jack Bailey was still a director but living in Cornwall. Mike Harley, came as a young boy to train and went on to be manager. I was by then a supervisor of the black and white department and processed and framed the 6 x 6 cm transparencies when they had to be individually mounted and bound around with black tape. I retired after 20 years, 24 counting those before the war.

We were very happy on the St Maurice estate where we lived for 44 years. We had three different houses there; first at 36 Hele, then 37 Erle to get a garage. The garden was quite small there and Bill was a very keen gardener, one day he met an engine driver who lived at 1 Hele Terrace. The traffic coming through was disturbing his sleep as he was on night shift work. At the same time there was another family who would like to move up to Erle to get a garage so one Saturday morning we had Nichols the movers up to do a three way switch. The television came up to film this happening. It was really funny, they took me last coming out of the house with the budgie in a cage and then speeded it all up.

Bill had very poor health due to arthritis and from 1970 had two artificial hips. Nevertheless he took part in all the Plympton St Maurice activities as secretary for the St Maurice Tenant's Association, and secretary for the old age pensioner's association. He was involved with the Gardening Association and the Civil Service Fellowship, the Dunkirk Veterans Association and the British Legion. His main hobby and interest was his garden and his greenhouse where he spent his time growing his tomatoes, cucumbers and loads of flowers. He had such patience to prick out thousands of tiny plants, most of which he gave away.

Bill died in July 1997 aged 88, the day before what would have been our 61st wedding anniversary. My father Herbert Hunwicks died in 1949, Mum died on Christmas day 1985. My friend Edie Cowlrick died in June 2002, my brother Ernie died in 2000 and sister Nell died on the 13th March 2003.

Stuarts Staff circa 1960
Standing, L to R: Mr Pomeroy, Ivy Cox, Michael.

Seated, L to R:?, Pat, Margaret, Marjorie, Lorna, Claudia, Lena, Doris, Mrs Smith.

We have come a long way since the war years when if we needed a new coat we bought a white blanket from Goulds and made one up. I now have two grandsons, Steven and Nick, a granddaughter Jenny and a great granddaughter, Kelly, who is fourteen now and they give me a lot of pleasure. I have had many adventures and much fun.

When Mum was 100. 14th September 1985.

Left to right
Ivy's brother Ernie, younger sister Betty, Ivy, sister Nell and Eddie.
Seated: Mrs Caroline Hunwicks.

Ivy at Stuarts. 1960.
Ivy now supervisor of the Black and White processing area checking the quality of prints.

Ivy with other staff. (4th from left). The large electric drum glazers in the right background are still in use at this time. 1960

EDDIE
Boyhood Memories

I was born on the 20th March, 1926, in 1 Beach Cottage beside Hooe Lake at Hooe, Plymouth, Devon.

The cottage was quite cramped, in fact I wondered how we all fitted in. There was no running water inside just a standpipe in the yard outside. All gas for cooking and lighting. Two rooms down, two rooms up. One of the downstairs rooms was the kitchen and living room. Upstairs there were two bedrooms, four children in one room and Mum and Dad with Betty, the youngest daughter, in the other.

Eddie Hunwicks age 4. 1930. in Hexton woods. The wall on the left is part of the old Chapel of St Anthony which was a private chapel for Radford House. It was demolished when the sewage works was built. Eddie is holding a bag full of conkers.

At 5 years of age I attended the infants section of Hooe and Turnchapel school in the adjoining village of Turnchapel. The seniors were up in what is now St John's Church Hall but a new school was being built in Hooe to combine both groups. The Turnchapel Infants school had just two rooms in a building where the ferry came in and the shore end of the ferry quay was the playground. That was 1931 and I was there for a year and then moved to the new school at the head of the lake in Hooe which had been completed in 1931.

For a small boy life in the village revolved around the lake, tide in or out, the nearby Hexton Woods or the beaches of Jennycliff and Bovisand some 10 and 45 minutes away respectively.

We explored the caves in Hexton Woods, using just bicycle lamps. There was an unfounded local story that the caves connected to Radford House and as that had been where Sir Water Raleigh had been placed under house arrest and considering his close association with gold and booty we thought, well, there might be something there. There were half a dozen of us, couple of girls too, we weren't much more than ten or eleven years old. We went down the entrance to the cave into a bit of a gallery where you could stand up and that's where the girls stayed while we went on through a little cleft in the gallery that opened into a natural passage. There had been a fall of stone that blocked the passage but there was a small hole in the floor which as kids we were able to get down and crawl along about six foot of a passage that opened up into an enormous cavern. You could barely see the top with our lights. The floor sloped down from there but the only way out that we could see was an opening high up in the wall that we couldn't get to. There was no treasure but we explored them again several times after that.

There was a circular yellow & black AA sign outside the school: It read 'Hooe (right across the middle)

Plymouth 4 miles. London 240 miles' We thought that a bit ironic as the chance of us going to London was very slim. It might as well have said so many miles to the moon for all it meant to us then as children.

We used to enjoy watching the stone barges load up with limestone from the two quarries at either end of Hooe Lake, Radford Quarry and Hooe Lake Quarry. There were two steel plate loading chutes at the Radford end, one by Hexton Quay and two at the western end of the lake for Hooe Lake Quarry. The barges would be moored up under the chute which was lowered down into its hold. Stone from the quarry was either brought out by horse and cart (Hooe Lake Quarry) or by tramway trucks. The carts had to be reversed up to the chute and the handlers were very good at getting their horses to back up until the carts' wheels hit a sleeper that was placed across the end of the chute. Then the cart was tipped over and all the stone rolled down the chute into the barge. This made a terrific noise, very dramatic.

Another place to explore and play was the rafts of timber that Bayly's timber yard made up to store the balks of timber until needed. We used to step from one to the other. You had to be careful you didn't fall in because the timber could close over

The Hooe Lake timber rafts were storage for 12" x 12" (305 mm x 305 mm) Baltic Pine that had been offloaded in Millbay Docks and floated around to Hooe Lake. Being substantial pieces of timber they would split if stored on land and allowed to dry out.

When needed they were floated down to the entrance of the lake where a spiked conveyor would pull them up out of the water to be sawn up and pressure treated for railway sleepers or telegraph poles.

Thanks to Roger Dawe who worked for Bayly's at Oreston.

Hooe Lake timber rafts circa 1930.
Photograph courtesy of Doreen Mole.

Timber raft limit balks 1930.
These came nearly up to the southern end of Hooe Lake. These limit balks were moored and the rafts floated loosely within them.

you. Also swans might be nesting and they got very protective.

Swimming was the main pastime, mostly off the quay. On one occasion we were on the quay talking and Ron Roberts had brought his bike along. We were joking about what it would be like to ride a bike off the end of the quay into the water. Anyway Ian Maddocks, who was a bit of a daredevil, took Ron's bike and rode it off the end of the quay into

Hooe Lake Timber Rafts. Circa 1928
Children playing on Bayly's timber floating from the west shore of Hooe Lake. Nos 1 and 2 Beach Cottages are in the background.
Reproduced by kind permission of Halsgrove Press.

Left to Right: Ernie, Eddie & Betty Hunwicks.

Ivy's brothers and sister taken by Ivy 1st July 1932 in Swift Studios, 37 Frankfort Street.

the water. Ian got out alright, laughing at Ron who was crying because he'd lost his bike. Well one of us dived down, put a rope around Ron's bike and we got it out, so that was OK, then Ian realised that he would have to go home to face his father and explain why all his clothes were soaking wet.

Ian's father was a bit of a golfer, well he had a set of clubs anyway. We boys used to make up golf clubs to play with, a bit of stick with something lashed to the end. Suddenly some of the lads had real clubs and it turned out that Ian had been sorting out his fathers clubs and exchanging them for a few sweets here and a comic there. His father was not pleased and demanded them all returned so Ian had to go round and get them back. We were adamant that the sweets were returned too, though we never got them back.

FOOD

We ate well, I don't remember being very hungry other than normal for a growing boy. My father did some of the cooking, he was a good cook, having learned in the Navy where each mess would cook its own meals, the sailors taking it in turns to do the cooking. You learned quickly like that as your mates would not be shy in letting you know your culinary shortcomings.

He used to make two particular dishes we had fairly regularly. One was 'Hoosh Teegoosh' which was layers of corned beef, sliced potatoes and onions. The final layer was potatoes. It was put in the oven and came out all nice and crisp on the top. A bit like a Lancashire Hotpot.

The other was 'Lash up and Stow' which was a sheet of suet pastry with onion and large pieces of bacon laid on it then rolled up like a Swiss Roll put into a pudding cloth, tied up and boiled for hours. It looked like a lashed up hammock, hence his name for it. When it was done it was sliced up. Lovely it was all suety and oniony.

Sticky Dinner was a favourite, leeks and things in it.

Sundays was invariably a roast meat. Chicken was few and far between and only for high days and holidays. Usually it was beef or lamb. Father would do the roast and put it in the oven then go and have his drink in the pub, which was only two doors away of course. He would come back in time for it to have been cooked, take it out of the oven and carve. He'd bring a jug of ale home for mother too. We ate in the kitchen.

Monday was cold from Sunday's roast as Mother was on the go with the washing.

There was a piano in the front room that father played. That was another Sunday routine. He would buy the News of the World because they would print half a sheet of music, usually of things like Flanagan and Allen songs and he'd pick this out on the piano. We'd have sing songs around the piano of course. My sisters Ivy and Nell had piano lessons from Eileen Coleman but by the time it got to us boys and my younger sister it had sort of died out. Dad did the prize crosswords from the News Chronicle, he won quite a few books from that.

When Ivy's fiancée Bill turned up, speaking with this strange Suffolk accent, we had rather mixed feelings. We did not want to lose Ivy but we could certainly use the room.

SHOPS

There was Harwoods, the Bakers in the centre of the square. They did general things too. Then later in the 1930's the Post Office and the butcher next door were built. Perry's had the Post Office and Bernard Stevens the butchers. There was another dairy, Phillips, that was set back on the main road just up from the Baptist Chapel. He kept his cows and did the milking at his farm at the bottom of Radford Dip.

Papers

Frank Rogers came around with newspapers. He had one of the £100 Ford Eights that were brought out in 1935/36 and the papers were loaded in the back and distributed to the paperboys from this. I did a paper round but I never had a local round. I was offered, and accepted, a round from Hooe to Wembury. There were only twelve papers to be delivered and I took them on a bike from Hooe. This was evenings after school but it didn't last very long because my father said that while he didn't mind if I did a local round he thought it a bit much riding out to Wembury on dark nights. Having a paper round was great because at that time there were boys comics like the Rover and the Wizard and they were always giving things away like little metal badges about football teams. Of course they often, er, fell out like and the paper boys would have these...

Local Employment

Main employment locally was at one of the two farms, the quarries or the timber yard. Otherwise the villagers worked in Turnchapel boatbuilding, Plymouth, Devonport Dockyard or joined the services.

Refuse Collection.

I cannot remember any refuse collection. There didn't seem to be a weekly collection like there is now. For instance the ashes we had from the fires were invariably used up on the allotments. Whatever you wanted to get rid seemed to end up in the lake.

One of the things they used to get rid of regularly into the lake were HT radio batteries. We had our first radio around 1927, a Cossor, it sat on a shelf in a small recess in the front room. To power the radio you needed an accumulator and a high tension battery, the top terminals of which were set in pitch. We used to make simple canoes and rafts and the like and seal the seams with bits of canvas and the pitch from these batteries. We'd heat them up in a pot and drain off the molten pitch. We used these canoes to go fishing in the Cattewater. The Turnchapel and Oreston Steamship Company, who ran the ferries, had some old hulks permanently moored up in the Cattewater that they used to store coal in. They had been there so long that the marine growth under them was very attractive to fish and we could catch fish quite easily off these. Small whiting it was mostly. There was that and prawning with a big flat hoop net. There were lots more prawns around in the entrance to Hooe Lake than there are now. Probably due to the sewage that came out!

Milk Round

When I was about nine years old I did a milk round before and after school for one of the farms, the milk being carried in pint cans and with one can hanging from each finger they were quite heavy to carry. If anyone wanted eggs or cream that was also put in a can and taken around and this was all before and after school each day. Mr Harris would do the milking and it would come into the Dairy with all bits and pieces that had fallen into the pail from the side of the cow. The only concession to hygiene at the farm was to pour the milk, straight from the milking pail, through a muslin gauze, into a churn from which it was measured into the cans. The milk was still warm from the cows and what a godsend on cold mornings for warming the fingers. My first work experience paid 6d (2.5p) per week.

Health

Mum used Sunlight soap for general washing and we used the red carbolic Lifebuoy soap to wash ourselves. Nits (head lice) were a problem, especially for the girls who had long hair. Mum used to put a sheet of paper on her lap and we would bend over it as she combed through our hair with a fine metal comb. The live nits fell onto the paper and mum cracked them between her thumbnails but the eggs were stuck onto the hair and this pulled dreadfully. We didn't have many because mum saw to it that we washed our hair regularly but we would catch them from other children. There was a treatment called Nursery Pomade which you could rub into your hair to kill nits but everyone knew you had been using it because your hair had a shiny look to it.

Doctors were very expensive and families would dread anyone getting sick. Jim Furze, who was the

> Nursery Pomade was an oil based lotion that attempted to kill nits by suffocation. Later treatments used DDT which was effective although, we know now, dangerous to the sufferer. Nits have now become resistant to DDT. The 2003 treatment uses Malathion insecticide but some head lice are are now immune to this too.

Landlord of the Royal Oak at that time, had been in the Navy as a medical orderly. As our nearest doctor was in Plymstock and expensive anyone with minor ailments, cuts, bruises and sprains would go to Jim Furze who gave them his advice, wrapped them up or whatever. He served a very useful purpose other than just landlord.

The Royal Oak was a Plymouth breweries pub. Bill Rowe, who had been a shipwright in the Navy, left the Navy and set up as a builder. He built Fanshawe Terrace and quite a lot of other houses. Well he enjoyed his drink and sometimes he would be a little 'over the top' shall we say. He was in the Royal Oak, one afternoon I think, anyway, it was outside of hours and Jim lost his licence. I think Bill might have felt a bit responsible, though he wasn't. Soon after Bill built the Hooe Social Club, called The Mountbatten Club, on the corner of Hooe Road and Lake road, where Harris Gardens is now, and installed Jim as its first landlord. Jim had some tragic luck really. His son Frank Furze was killed very early in the war.

BLACKSHIRTS

In about 1936 a large motor cruiser come into the lake tied up to the quay and disgorged half-a-dozen large fellows dressed in black uniforms with leather belts and high boots. They were accompanied by a fierce looking Alsatian dog that our local dogs certainly didn't like the look of. They probably had the right instincts for the men were members of the Plymouth Fascist party on a recruiting drive. We children ware fascinated because their speeches were greeted with much barracking from the assembled crowd. Several of these meetings were held but as far as I know only one person joined and donned the uniform and he promptly went into the Army as soon as war was declared.

MORE SCHOOL

While I was at Hooe School the government changed the school system. School leaving age was 14 and children had been at the same school from infants to 14. Now there was to be a split at eleven so when I was 11 years of age I went to the senior school at Plymstock about two miles distant, but not for long. My brother, four years my senior, had, in 1934, gone to Greenwich school, which in fact was not at Greenwich as it had moved in 1932 to a new site at Holbrook in Suffolk. He would arrive home at holiday times in a smart naval uniform which besides thrilling the local girls also enthralled me and as a result, in 1938, at 12 years of age I followed in his footsteps.

In June, 1938, I was put on a train in Plymouth by a tearful Mum and Dad (and me) and despatched

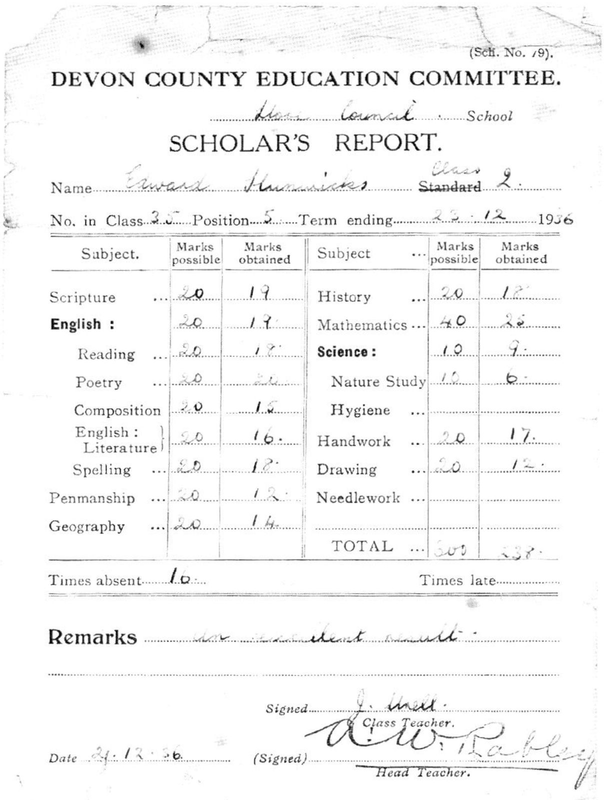
(Sch. No. 79).

DEVON COUNTY EDUCATION COMMITTEE.

Hooe Council School

SCHOLAR'S REPORT.

Name Edward Hunwicks Class ~~Standard~~ 2.

No. in Class 35 Position 5 Term ending 23.12 1936

Subject.	Marks possible	Marks obtained	Subject	Marks possible	Marks obtained
Scripture	20	19	History	20	18
English :	20	19	Mathematics	40	25
Reading	20	18	Science :	10	9
Poetry	20	20	Nature Study	10	6
Composition	20	15	Hygiene		
English : Literature	20	16	Handwork	20	17
Spelling	20	18	Drawing	20	12
Penmanship	20	12	Needlework		
Geography	20	14			
			TOTAL	300	238

Times absent 16 Times late

Remarks an excellent result.

Signed J. Uhell. Class Teacher.

Date 24.12.36 (Signed) A. W. Pabley Head Teacher.

HOOE COUNCIL SCHOOL

ATHLETIC SPORTS, 1937

100 Yards Boys Under 13

1st Edward Hunwicks

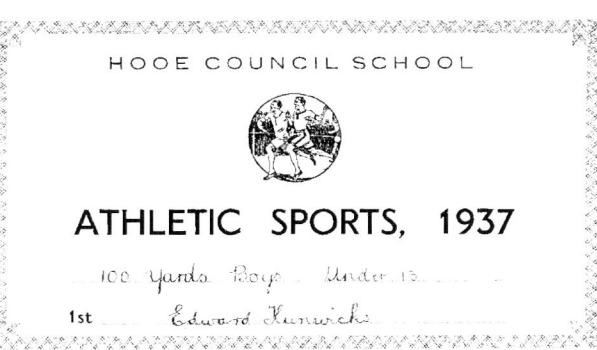

to Paddington in the care of the guard en route to Holbrook. There was a further exam to take and an overnight stop at Greenwich where we were looked after by old, positively ancient from our stand-point, Naval pensioners. I remember having supper there and being supplied with a drink in a basin, not a cup. We couldn't decide what the liquor was so I asked, Oliver Twist like, "Please Sir, is this tea or coffee?" This resulted in my first Naval reprimand and in effect I was told that if I didn't get any worse than that in the Navy I could consider myself very lucky. I never did find out whether it was tea or coffee. There were 800 boys at Holbrook aged from 12 to 15 split into ten houses all named after famous admirals and I was placed in St Vincent House.

When war started in 1939, keeping scrap-books became quite a popular hobby and each house had

*Eddie Hunwicks with carnival bike. 1937
Dressed in his older brother's uniform and holding his bicycle that he decorated for the Hooe Carnival.*

a plentiful supply of newspapers and periodicals including the Sphere and the Illustrated London News, the pictures from these were avidly collected to adorn the scrap-books.

For ceremonial occasions and going on holiday we wore Naval Blue jackets uniform complete with cap bands emblazoned ROYAL HOSPITAL SCHOOL. Anyone wanting to read the full title had to more or less circumnavigate the wearer of the cap. At the start of the war, for security reasons, Naval ratings no longer exhibited the ship's name on their caps but had the abbreviation HMS. Not to be outdone we cut up the cap ribbons extracted the 'RHS' and stuck this on our caps. Needless to say this was done out of sight of the school.

Holiday time could never come soon enough and the days were ticked off the calendars, shoes polished for hours on end to achieve a mirror-finish and bell-bottoms trouser legs pressed concertina fashion to acquire the desired ladder effect.

When going on holiday before the war started we would be taken by bus early in the morning to Ipswich, then by train to Liverpool Street, tube to Paddington then train again to Plymouth and home. At the outbreak of war it was decided that the boys should all arrive home in daylight hours so those who lived in far-away places left school in the afternoon before leave day. Cornwall was considered far away but not Devon. Presented with this challenge I managed to persuade the Division Officer that after arriving at Plymouth I had to catch the ferry to get home, so would arrive in the dark. He seemed to remember a ferry did in fact go to Turnchapel and so I joined he Cornwall boys and left the day before. I didn't of course admit that there was a perfectly good bus service which would get me home in ample time. The logic of this travel routine still escapes me as it meant we arrived at Paddington in the early evening and had to catch the midnight train from there to Plymouth, leaving us to wander around London for several hours. Fortunately no bombs fell at that time and the railway men at Paddington gave us an open invitation to use their canteen, as they did with real servicemen. I don't really think they were taken in by our RHS cap ribbons.

One popular hobby at school was fretwork from which a whole range of useful items were produced from plywood such as letter racks and pipeholders. In 1940 I was in the middle of producing a plaque that depicted symbolic figures of Britain and France with the caption 'Britain and France. United We Stand' when France fell!

The fall of France and danger of invasion concentrated the minds of the school authorities and it was decided to send home all those boys who lived in safe areas, Plymouth being amongst them would you beleive! In June 1940 back I came to Hooe and signed up with a school in Plymouth to restart my studies in preparation for the RN Artificers Apprentices

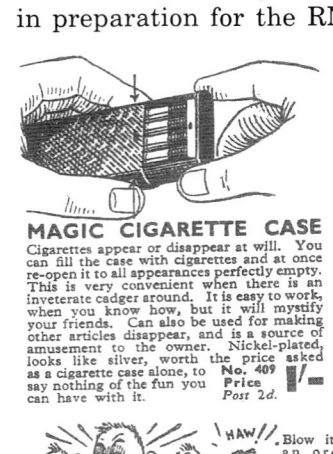

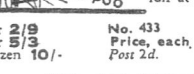
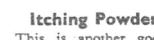

*Ellisdon's Advert 1938.
Ellisdon & Son was a mail order firm based at 246 High Holborn, London, specialising in tricks and novelties. They closed circa 1975. Eddie admits to Stink Bombs and Itching Powder.*

Entry exam in April 1941. The four miles to school I travelled by bike and when the bombs fell on the town my route often had to be diverted owing to rubble strewn streets.

In August 1940 high explosive and incendiary bombs were dropped on the village so in October building of an air raid shelter commenced. On the night of 27 November bombs fell on the village killing ten people and also set fire to some naval oil storage tanks on the opposite side of the lake to us. The fire lasted three days and was a target for other bombs during this time. On the 28th November a tank exploded and spilled oil caught alight on the lake. We were all evacuated to the next village for a few days in case more explosions followed. My sister's house in the village was severely damaged and two people next door to her were killed, though my sisters were safe. Dozens of incendiary bombs failed to explode and could be seen in the lake when the tide went out. We boys waded out and collected them to line them up on the quay to be removed by the ARP, but not quite all of them as we each managed to retain souvenir.

The construction of these bombs was quite easily seen from the partially exploded ones and it was a simple matter to unscrew the detonator, which we did. I had a detonator, a copper disc like one of today's watch batteries, until my mother found out and very wisely passed it over to the ARP.

A few weeks prior to the oil tank bombing the local ferryman, who ran a small ferry across to Oreston at the entrance to the Lake, found a half submerged rowing boat and salvaged it for sale at £2 10 shillings (£2.50). My school friend and I reached an agreement with him to buy it at one shilling a week.

We used it for a while until we discovered that we were bailing more than we were rowing so we pulled it up on the quay for repairs. The leaking joints were sealed by melted pitch from the tops of those old discarded wireless HT batteries, of which there was still an ample supply in the Lake. Repairs were well in progress when the bombing occurred again and an incendiary went right through the bow. Fortunately it didn't catch the boat alight but made a massive hole.

My school was near the War Damage Claims Office so I dropped in to fill out a claim form only to be told that five pounds was the minimum that could be claimed. However the Claims Officer said that although we had only paid £2.10s perhaps it was really worth £5. I readily agreed.

As we were shortly due to be paid £5 I approached the ferryman and suggested that we suspend instalments as he would soon be paid a lump sum from my compensation. He then told me that his ferryboat had also been hit and completely destroyed in the raids. However as he could neither read nor write he could not fill in the claim form. If I made the claim form out for him he would let me off the balance owed. This I did and I recall he claimed £18 as his boat was his 'sole means of livelihood'. He made his mark on the form and I took it to the office personally and told them the story. This was in about 1940. How he got on I do not know as I never saw him again but in 1943 a cheque arrived for me from the claims office for £5.

Bomb damage to our cottage resulted in our move to another village about two miles away and I continued my schooling. There were further periodic raids but none affected my family personally. In April 1941 I passed my entrance exams and on the 14th August 1941 entered the Navy at HMS Fisguard.

Left to right: Eddie, Herbert (Dad) and Ernie Cox.
Taken in 1943 outside 29 Manor Road.
Eddie was an artificer,
Ernie was invalided out in 1944.

WASHDAY

For Mrs Hunwicks the process of hand washing using a copper was tedious and time consuming. First stubborn stains were hand rubbed with Sunlight soap on a ridged washboard. All whites were then boiled in the copper with about half a teacup of washing soda for around ten minutes. They would have to be moved around with a stick to get evenly washed and it was important not to overload the copper so there was some room for movement. The

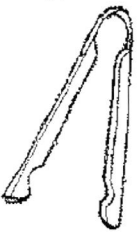 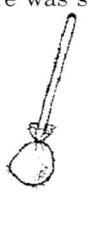 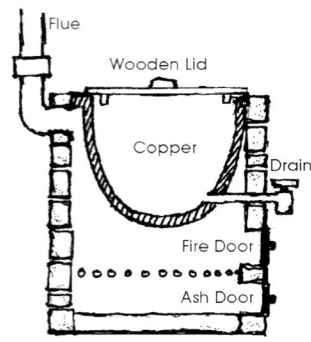

hot clothes were removed from the copper with a large pair of wooden tongs and given two rinses in cold water, with a mangling in between. A final separate rinse had a blue bag swished into it to give the whites a blue tinge. This counteracted the yellowing to which white linens and cottons are prone and made them look bright white. A final mangle and then hung up to dry. Only the best Coppers were actually made out of copper. Usually they were cast iron and did not have a drain tap. These were emptied by bailing them out with a bowl. The mangle was shared between the two cottages and stood against the wall covered with a tarpaulin

when not in use. To press clothes an iron was heated on the gas stove. Then a polished, clean metal shield, or 'shoe', was slipped over the sole so it did not mark the cloth and slid over it easily.

Reckitt's Blue was an artificial ultramarine consisting of a silicate of sodium and aluminium with sodium sulphite. The powdered synthetic ultramarine was mixed with sodium carbonate and corn starch then compressed into a tablet. This would dye anything it came in contact with and was often supplied in a little muslin bag on the end of a stick so the rinse water could be coloured up without the need to touch the concentrated dye. Reckitt's Blue has been used in its concentrated form as a dye and decorative paint. There was no single formula for laundry blue, or Dolly Blue, as it was made by a variety of manufacturers but the name 'Reckitt's Blue' was popularly adopted for all makes as Reckitt were the initiator and the largest manufacturer. Rather like Mr. Biro and his pen. Reckitt's ceased manufacture of Blue in the 1950's. The advent of detergents and washing machines brought about a collapse in demand. Modern detergents have an ultra-violet light sensitive additive to make whites bright.

Isaac Reckitt was born in Wainfleet in 1792 one of nine children in a strongly Quaker family. It was through the group's many meetings he met his future wife, Anne Colby, whom he married in 1819 in Boston, Lincs. The couple set up their home in St Anne's Terrace. Isaac was in the milling business with his brother but the business failed to support them. Recovering from a serious illness he and his wife made the decision to leave the mill. They moved to Nottingham where they went into the corn industry milling corn flour. However this did not prosper and mounting debts forced them to look elsewhere. The collapse of the business turned out to be a blessing in disguise as the couple bought a starch works in Hull where they prospered creating a variety of starch based products, mainly laundry starch and stove blacking. Isaac died in 1862 and his sons diversified further creating the famous Reckitt's Blue, disinfectants (Lysol) and metal polishes (Brasso and Silvo). The business went from strength to strength and eventually the whole family were employed. The company then joined forces with the Colman empire who were also, originally, starch millers and who had discovered that by adding mustard flour to corn flour it made a very palatable condiment.

As employers the Reckitt family were paternalistic, in the best sense of the word, looking after their employees with subsidized food, health care, pension and housing. Those that worked in the blue factory were so covered in blue dye that they had a special bus to take them home. In 1907 a workers village was started, Reckitt's Garden Village in East Hull, which still has its own identity. Architecturally it was heavily influenced by the arts and crafts movement and the garden theme carried through into streets named after trees. It was mostly completed by 1914.

References
Reckitt, The History of Reckitt and Sons Ltd.
'The Backbarrow Ultramarine Works Company' by Mike Davies-Shiel in the CIHS Bulletin, December 2000.
Stanford University USA.

Visit the garden village on www.tenfoot.karoo.net/garden.html and www.hullcc.gov.uk/hullinprint/archive.

SEWAGE

Numbers one and two Beach Cottages were, when built, connected to main drains for sewage and waste water. However this was not quite the main drains as we think of them today, though they did have a flush toilet.

The cottages in Hooe village are either built on an excavated quarry floor or on the limestone bluff. This makes for a sound foundation but is difficult to dig away for a septic tank or cess pit. In any case the cottages around the shore have little ground. This meant that many householders would use buckets which were taken down and emptied into the lake. This was not only inconvenient but decidedly unsanitary, especially if the tide was out.

Much better, it was reasoned, to build one large communal sewage holding tank in a place where this would be simpler to construct and where the contents of which could easily be disposed.

The solution was to extend the quay by building a large concrete tank on the end and connecting all the cottages to this. To dispose of the sewage a syphon system was installed and connected to an outflow pipe that ran over the surface of the mud to a point approximately midway across the lake. The capacity of the tank and the height of the syphon were calculated so that the sewage from the village would only leave the tank on ebbing tides.

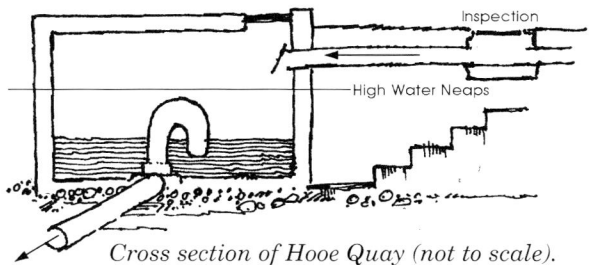
Cross section of Hooe Quay (not to scale).

As the tide came in it flowed up the outflow pipe into the tank and filled the tank to the same level as the tide. As the tide went out so did the contents of the tank, the lowest portions syphoning out until the tank was almost empty again. It was thought that the tide and the freshwater streams flowing into Hooe Lake would take it away to the Cattewater, then the Plym flow would carry it to the Sound and then out to sea. What we might consider as being a rather thoughtless attitude towards dumping raw sewage into the sea and the ability of the sea to dispose of it was considered as being quite acceptable and the acme of modern sanitation.

(Recent hydrographic surveys have shown that there is a considerable eddying process between the Sound, the Cattewater and the Tamar and that little is actually washed out to sea, quite a lot returns on the next tide. Much as locals have long suspected.)

This detritus fed fish and crustaceans and many locals will attest that the prawn population has fallen considerably since the new sewage treatment works was brought on line. Local children often swam in the lake, apparently risking typhoid, dysentery, diarrhoea and cholera but the remembered incidence of illness seems low and many would say that their immune system was toughened up by the experience. In 2003 the Water Supply and Sanitation Collaborative Council estimated that one gramme of untreated human faeces can contain 10m viruses, 1m bacteria, 1,000 parasite cysts and 100 worm eggs.

The mechanics of the system worked fairly well, until the quantity of sewage entering the tank exceeded the designed heights of the syphon, then it poured out whatever the state of the tide. As further development occurred in Hooe and more water was used this is what happened with increasing frequency.

Consequently in 1964/65 a new treatment works was built in Hexton Woods with a pumping station and holding tanks on the newly infilled southern end of Hooe Lake. Local sewage is piped to the holding tanks from where it is pumped to the treatment works. From here the treated water flows into the lake and the solids are collected by boat and taken out to sea to be dumped.

The line of the old sewage outlet pipe can still be seen in stones extending from Hooe Quay.

SLOE GIN

There are many recipes for making Sloe Gin but they only seem to vary slightly in the quantities, not the ingredients.

Sloe Gin is a delicious drink, warming and fruity for those cold winter evenings.

The Plymouth Gin company sell a ready made version, which is most acceptable, but you do not have the sense of achievement you get from making your own.

You do not have to use Plymouth Gin as a base but, hey, this is a local recipe, it is stronger than most other gin and has a distinctive flavour that goes well with sloes.

Ingredients
1 bottle (70 cl/700 ml/1.25 pints) of Plymouth Gin.
450 grams (1lb) of sloes
170 grams (6 ozs) of granulated sugar

You will need a 2.5litre (1.5pint) sealable leakproof container large enough to hold all this. A Kilner Jar, Le Pratique or similar preserving jar is excellent as the mouth is wide enough to get the sloes in easily.
You will also need patience as the process takes about three months.

Process
Wash the sloes well. When fresh they have a natural bloom on the skin. This does not have to be removed.

Prick each sloe all over with a darning needle or fine knitting needle. The idea is to break the skin to allow the juices and gin to intermingle*.

Place the washed sloes in your container, add the sugar and pour in the Gin. Fix the top on tightly so it is leakproof and give it a good shake to dissolve and distribute the sugar and gin. Not all the sugar will dissolve at first.

Every day give the container a shake in the morning and again in the evening. Do this for three weeks then leave the container in a cool, dark place for at least ten more weeks. Have a look at it occasionally to admire the deepening ruby red colour.

The longer you leave it the better it is but six months is more than enough. Three is usual so you drink it at Christmas time.

Decanting
The aim is to get the liquid as clear as possible. A two stage process is most effective:
Stage one: Sieve the contents through a coarse flour sieve and squeeze the residue with a wooden spoon. Discard the residue**.
Stage two: Pass the liquid through coffee filter papers or a fine muslin cloth.
Bottle and cork securely. Store in a cool dark place after you have had a little tashte jusht t' sheck itsh kwalty.

Drinking
Sloe Gin should be regarded as a liqueur and taken neat in small amounts, with or without ice, after dinner. It is also excellent drizzled over vanilla ice cream and added to the ice cream mix if you have an ice cream maker.

Sloes are the fruit of the Blackthorn (prunus spinosa) which grows in hedges and copses throughout England and Europe. The name Blackthorn is derived from the thin branches which are black or dark grey and some of the smaller branches develop into thorns. It has masses of small white flowers around April/May before the leaves come out and this gives it its other name of White May. The fruit is round, about 15 mm in diameter with a black skin and a single stone in the middle. Eaten raw they have a very bitter taste.

Sloes are ripe in late September and on into October. Some say that they should be picked after the first frosts as the freezing improves the flavour.

* As a variation to the pricking process try freezing your washed sloes then putting them in a strong bag and hitting them with a wooden mallet or rolling pin to break the skins. It is not necessary to smash them to pieces. Then proceed as above.

** Try adding a bottle of Vodka to the residue and leaving it for about three weeks.

DALMENY HOUSE

Dalmeny House is the Tudor-revival home of the Earls of Rosebery. Although the estate has belonged to the Primrose family since 1662, Barnbougle Castle was the family residence until Dalmeny House was built by the English architect William Wilkins in 1817.

Dalmeny was the first Tudor-revival house to be built in Scotland, featuring octagonal towers, mullion and transom windows and carved chimney-pots. Inside the hammer-beamed hall, stained-glass windows and fan-vaulted corridors are distinctly Gothic but the other rooms adopted the regency fashion of the time.

The marriage of the Archibald Primrose, the 3th Earl, (1847 - 1929) to Hannah the daughter of the Baron Meyer de Rothschild resulted in major sections of the Rothschild Collection of art and furniture coming to Dalmeny to join the existing Rosebery Collection. The result is an important collection of 18th Century French furniture, Goya tapestries, porcelain, paintings and other objects d'Art, together with a collection of Burn's memorabilia. The paintings include portraits by Gainsborough, Raeburn, Reynolds and Lawrence, which are displayed in the Dining Room. The Napoleon Room contains one of the world's most important Napoleonic collections, paintings of the emperor, furniture used by him and other trophies assembled by the fifth Earl of Rosebery, such as the Duke of Wellington's campaign chair.

Dalmeny was damaged by a fire during World War II, but was sympathetically restored and played a part in the conception of the Edinburgh Festival, thanks to the enthusiasm of both the 6th Earl and Countess. Today Dalmeny remains the home of the 7th Earl of Rosebery, having been opened to the public in 1979.

CINEMAS

Between 1918 and 1950 the holiday, resident and combined Services population of Plymouth provided massive support for the cinema. Centered mainly around Union Street cinemas were being rapidly converted from halls and theatres, competition was fierce and demand, it seemed, was insatiable and as yet unaffected by television.

'In the 1930's there were 250,000 cinema seats a week and the Western Evening Herald was reviewing sixteen cinemas every Tuesday' (Gill 1993)

Following their history is complex as they burned down, were demolished, bombed and frequently were taken over and had their names changed. Here I have singled out three that Ivy particularly mentions and to some extent their fates and fortunes mirror the others.

The Electric

At 3pm on Friday July 29th 1910 the 400-seat Empire Electric opened at 40 Union Street, Plymouth, between Station Road and Buckland Place. Admission cost 6d or 3d and the adverts proclaimed 'Only latest pictures shown' and 'Come when you like...Leave when you like'. A licence was granted for the theatre to Mr R E Wensley, manager of the above-named company, at the end of August. It was one of the few cinemas in the area where the screen was located over the entrance to the auditorium.

The interior was decorated in a warm shade of crimson with green hangings and it was lit with red and white electric lamps. The upholstered seats were of the tip-up type. The atmosphere was kept cool by what the Western Morning News termed 'an electric contrivance'. Externally the theatre was white and gold and 'the smartly uniformed porter is by no means an insignificant feature', continued the local press.

However, the most noteworthy feature was the use of an Anamatiphone by means of which the film was synchronized with a gramophone, 'thus rendering it possible to reproduce both the music and the spectacular effects and acting of an entire opera'. Thus for the remainder of the first week eight scenes from "Faust" were both seen and heard, occupying about forty minutes. Other operas were to follow.

Sadly, things went very wrong and a notice appeared in the Western Daily Press on the following day apologising for the 'temporary failure of the machines' and the sudden termination of the afternoon performance but adding that the evening show was 'greatly appreciated by a large audience'. Those patrons who had received complimentary tickets were invited to 'favour the Theatre with another visit'. (Moseley 2002)

Evidently Mrs Dalton's services as a pianist were still needed

The New Palladium

The story of the New Palladium is worth telling in more detail as it illustrates very well the establishment of a cinema in the 20's. Also its owner/manager and his daughter were interesting characters...

Reuben Eady circa 1931.

Reuben and Caroline Eady and their daughter, Dorothy, lived in the London suburb of Blackheath.

Reuben was trained as a master tailor but was also a part-time magician and conjuror, working small clubs, cabaret and music halls under the name of Brandon Dalmar. However Reuben was becoming increasingly disillusioned with his career as a tailor and in 1919, at the age of 40, became convinced that movies were going to be a really lucrative form of entertainment.

He took his family on a tour of the the UK, looking for buildings that could be converted into cinemas. He found what he wanted in Plymouth, on Ebrington Street, a skating rink and dance hall called The American Roller Rink. He persuaded a London consortium, the Parliament Picture House Company Ltd, to provide him with the funds necessary to convert this into a cinema. This involved the addition of a projection room and balcony. So enthused was he that it is said that he laid many of the bricks himself.

The New Palladium held a seated audience of 3,500 with another 1,000 standing. The projection room was a hundred and fifty feet away from the screen, making it necessary for the projectionist to use binoculars in order to focus the film. The roof was corrugated iron, which did make it rather noisy when it rained hard but audiences did not seem to notice. After all in some of the cinemas in Union Street parts of the lower floor would flood on high spring tides.

Reuben Eady was a short, rather tubby but imposing and imperious figure who was always well dressed and who kept a pair of scissors in his pocket to extract butts from a cigarette holder that he used to place between his lips while turning his head in profile to his audience.

The doors first opened on Monday December 11th 1922 at 6.30. The movie Reuben. Eady chose to inaugurate his cinema was Erich von Stroheim's 'Foolish Wives'. It ran for two weeks, with more than 3,000 viewers attending each performance. The New Palladium was an immediate success and Reuben Eady became renowned as a 'manager extraordinaire.' During the summer months he had huge blocks of ice placed at various locations inside the cinema in order to make it 'the coolest theatre in town.' He also installed an 'electrical vapour machine' that not only made the building smell like a cathedral but also served to disinfect the cinema.

The New Palladium also housed the first cinema organ in Plymouth - 'The Home of the Pipe Organ,' as the advertisements put it - which was used both for accompanying the silent movies and for occasional solo organ recitals. Three times a week a Plymouth orchestra would broadcast performances 'live from the New Palladium' over the local BBC radio station.

On Friday nights and as prologues and interludes to the films, Eady would devise, produce, and direct his own concerts and dramatic spectacles. On one occasion Eady presented three girls dancing on roller skates in front of a pirate ship in full sail.

Another time gaudily dressed American Indians in war paint rushed onto the stage to attack a group of covered wagons, while a musician jumped up from the pit and charged after the assailants, wildly firing blank shots at them.

In a memorable tableau vivant, the head of a demon, with horns and flashing eyes, stared down ominously at three ghostly figures who were flitting around a huge fire.

At calmer moments there would be a musical interlude, during which a buxom girl named Dorothy Lincoln would appear on stage dressed exotically and sing a popular music-hall number, embellishing her performance with a full range of melodramatic gesticulations to the accompaniment of a fifteen-piece orchestra.

Dorothy Eady in 1920 aged 16.

Dorothy Lincoln was the stage name for Reuben Eady's daughter. A resident of Plymouth recalled: "Dorothy was a large girl and quite good-looking in those days. I well remember the prologue to the film 'The Thief of Bagdad', starring Douglas Fairbanks. Just before the movie began, Dorothy Lincoln appeared on stage wearing an oriental costume and proceeded to give a rendition of 'Somewhere in the Sahara', a popular song at the time, though Reuben changed it for the occasion to 'Somewhere in Old Baghdad'. Reuben Eady would stand at the back of the theatre applauding wildly after each song and just daring anybody to respond unappreciatively when Dorothy was performing on stage."

It seems that Dorothy had talent for she also worked with a local theatre group. However she became famous in her own right for another reason. At the age of three she fell downstairs and from that moment was convinced that she was the reincarnation of Omm Sety, the temple priestess and lover of the 19th Dynasty Pharoah Sety 1. Her wholehearted belief and committment to this was remarkable and she became a renowned Egyptian scholar. She died in 1981 and her life is documented in 'The Search for Omm Sety' by Jonathon Cott, from which this account of her father has been edited.

Eady was, according to his former projectionist, a 'fair and straight-speaking man.' Now genteel middle-class, Reuben Eady was one of the first residents of Plymouth to own a car. He eventually moved his family from their flat over the cinema to an opulent trailer in the nearby countryside.

1929 saw the arrival of sound films. The New Palladium was bought by Denham Picture Houses (later a part of the Rank Organisation), which kept him on as manager of both the New Palladium and the Savoy in Union Street. In 1931 he became manager of the new Gaumont Cinema on the corner of Union Street and Flora Street.

In this new age of talkies Reuben Eady's flamboyant directorial skills and theatrical flair were no longer appreciated or needed. In 1934 he gave up the film business completely, having lost his enthusiasm for what was now mostly administrative work. He suffered increasingly from bouts of severe depression and died in his caravan, ten years before his wife, on May 28, 1935, at the age of fifty-six.

The New Palladium cinema was bombed in March of 1941 and not rebuilt.
(Cott 1987)

The Regent after fully converting to the Odeon.

The Regent

On Saturday November 21st 1931, the Regent in Frankfort Street opened very close to Swift Studios and the Western Morning News. The decor was aluminium and ivory and it had a seating capacity of 3,500, of which 1,390 were in the balcony; one of the ten largest cinemas in Europe. There was a large waiting area furnished with deep-sprung couches to enable tickets to be sold in advance to 2,000 people who could then be let into the auditorium as quickly as the previous audience was leaving. In front of the curtains were placed three fairy water fountains. An HMV Panatrope system provided the incidental music although there was room for an orchestra.

Admission prices: Up to 4pm: 2,500 seats at 7d and 1,000 seats at 1s. After 4pm: front ground floor 7d; back ground floor 1s; front circle 2s; back circle 1s 6d.

The opening film, shared with the Hippodrome in Devonport, was Charlie Chaplin in "City Lights" which most people had not realised was a silent film with only sound effects and music. Attendance to this was much boosted by the publicity surrounding the visit to Plymouth earlier in the week of its star. He had spent two days in Plymouth as the guest of Lady Astor. Although he did make a brief appearance on the stage at the Palace Theatre he left on the night train for London and so was not involved with the opening of the Regent. (Moseley 2002)

> There is much fascinating information about the cinemas of Plymouth on Brian Moseley's website www.plymouthdata.info to which I am indebted for the above quotes. He has also written the excellent 'Plymouth Through the Lens' series that may be obtained through local booksellers or from himself at 15 Watts Park Road, Plymouth PL2 3NN

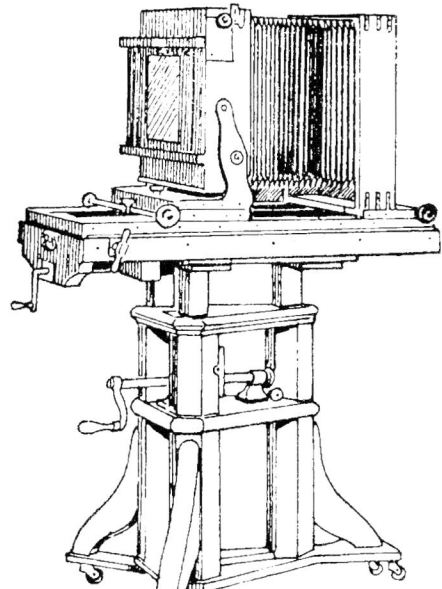

Studio camera of the type used by Ivy at Swift Studio. It took a card negative 10.5 x 5.5 inches on which they took three photos 3.5 x 5.5 inches side by side

PHOTOGRAPHY

From 1900 until 1950 Plymouth was one of the largest centres of film and photography useage with most of the theatres and studios being grouped in and around Union street.

In his book 'Union Street' Chris Robinson writes: 'At the end of the nineteenth century two thirds of the main photographers of the three towns were based in Union Street...In 1898 there were nine based in the Stonehouse section of the strip, between Manor Street and St Mary street and another five in the Plymouth section.'

Plymouth was both an important services town and a holiday venue so there was a steady business in picture postcards and Developing and Printing (D&P) as well as for pictures of loved ones leaving for tours of duty. Servicemen and women added to the local fixed and transient population to supply huge audiences for some massive cinemas and theatres. Home entertainments such as Radio and Television were not competitors, as yet.

These studios were commercial users of film and photography but Plymouth does have one claim to fame in the field of photographic invention, albeit an ultimately unsuccessful one. William Friese-Green had studied photography with Fox Talbot and set up a studio in Union Street in 1880. However he was more interested in making moving pictures and spent his time, and money, on trying to perfect a movie system. He experimented with lantern slides shown in quick succession (This was doomed as a lantern slide was 83 mm square, 3 mm thick, weighed 51 grams and was made of two pieces of glass. Getting a stack of these to move in sequence through a projector at sufficient speed to give the illusion of movement for a satisfactory length of time was, to put it mildly, challenging.) He also tried with images on celluloid and worked with two other engineers to perfect a 'machine camera' and projector. He gave up the studio in Plymouth and moved to Bath and then London but despite having all the basic principles the technology of the time let him down as did possible investors in his ideas. A plaque to his memory was on the wall of the Two Trees Public House at the town end of Union Street.

RAAF
10 Squadron

Australian Sunderland crew, Mount Batten circa 1941.
Standing second from left: Bill.
Seated L to R: Burt, Curly.

The first Royal Australian Airforce squadron to go operational was No. 10. The original intention was that the crews came to England, just before the outbreak of war, to take delivery of a number of Sunderland Flying Boats that were being converted to Australian specifications then ferry them back to Australia.

Such is the nature of things they stayed, operating the flying boats from Mount Batten for the duration of the war, fighting as a unit of RAF Coastal Command where they patrolled coastal waters spotting UBoats and any other possibly unfriendly craft. There is a memorial to them on the side of Mount Batten Tower.

Joe Leach
Flew with 10 Squadron and 113 Air Sea Rescue in the South Pacific. He has written 'RAAF Flying Boats at War, the way it was'.

Wing Commander Donald Bennet.
Became commander of 10 Squadron in April 1942 and took part in the raid on the Tirpitz. He was shot down but evaded capture and eventually arrived home via Sweden.

HMT DUNERA

HMT Dunera. The ship in which Bill sailed to Malta in 1937.

HMT Dunera was built in 1937 and owned by the British India Steam Navigation Company. She was capable of a cruising speed of 16 knots and had accommodations for about 1400 people including crew. When Bill sailed on her to Malta she was a new ship. Throughout the War she was used as a troop transport and is best known for the infamous Dunera Boys incident which took place in 1940.

In May and June 1940, 75,000 refugees from Germany and Austria, mostly Jewish, were rounded up in Britain. Threatened by a German invasion, Winston Churchill insisted that the German-speaking Jews might well be supporters of Hitler and he wanted them out of the country.

Some were put aboard HMT Dunera at Liverpool together with Nazi army and naval prisoners, 200 Italian fascists, German merchant marine prisoners that survived the torpedoing of the Arandora Star prison ship by the Germans (and were the survivors of the 2000 captives that went down with that ship) and a number of other Italians.

The British guards aboard the Dunera were advised that they were all dangerous enemy soldiers, sailors and spies and subjected them to humiliation and brutality. Living conditions aboard were dreadful even without the brutal treatment. The ships capacity was 1400 and there were now 2,732 plus crew and guards. The ship sailed for Australia, who had agreed to take them and put them in a prisoner of war camp in Woomera. It arrived on September 6th 1940.

The atrocious behavior of the guards and the conditions of the voyage were hushed up and the Home Office put the papers on the Dunera case on a 100-year embargo.

Among the Dunera boys, as they became known, were composer Felix Werder, actor Max Bruch, political scientists Henry Mayer and Hugo Wolf, athletics trainer Franz Stampfl, anthropologist Leonhard Adam, artist Ludwig Hirschfeld-Mac, who'd taught at the Bauhaus, economist Fred Greun, art historian Franz Philipp, film-maker Kurt Sternburg, physicist Hans Kronenburger, judge Stephen Strauss and mathematician Felix Behrend.

There is an Australian film The Dunera Boys (1985) starring Bob Hoskins and Joseph Spano.

The Dunera was broken up in 1967.

For more details see:
www.peoplesvoice.gov.au/stories/nsw/hay_m_pow.htm

Paul R. Bartrop with Gabrielle Eisen, The Dunera Affair
(Schwartz & Wilkinson, Melbourne, 1990).

Peter & Leni Gillman, Collar the Lot: How Britain Interned and Expelled Its Wartime Refugees (Quartet Books Ltd., London, 1980).

Benzion Patkin, The Dunera Internees (Cassell Australia Ltd.,
Melbourne, 1979).

Cyril Pearl, The Dunera Scandal (Angus & Robertson, Sydney, 1983).

NAP

NAP rules
With thanks to John McLeod

Nap, or Napoleon, is a trick taking game in which players receive five cards each. Whoever bids the highest number of tricks chooses trumps and tries to win at least that many. It first appeared in the late 19th century. It may be less popular now than it was, but it is still played in some parts of southern England. It is usual to play for small stakes and settle up after each hand.

Players and cards
Nap can be played by as few as three players, but it is better with four or more. There are no permanent partnerships; in each hand the high bidder plays against a team consisting of all the other players.

A standard 52 card pack is used, the cards in each suit ranking from high to low: A-K-Q-J-10-9-8-7-6-5-4-3-2. Formerly it was played with the full pack, but nowadays many players prefer to reduce the pack by taking out the low cards of each suit, so reducing the number of undealt cards. For example three players might play with 24 cards (A-K-Q-J-10-9), four with 28 (from ace down to 8) and five with 32 (ace down to seven).

Deal
In most schools the cards are shuffled only at the start of the game and after a successful bid of 5 (Nap) or above. Otherwise they are just gathered together and cut by the player to dealer's right. The dealer deals five cards to each player - a batch of three each followed by a batch of two each, or two each followed by three each.

Deal and play are clockwise, and the turn to deal passes to the left after each hand.

Bidding
The bidding starts with the player to dealer's left, goes around the table clockwise and ends with the bidder. Each player has just one chance to speak and at your turn you must either pass or bid more than the highest bid so far. The possible bids, in ascending order, are:

Three - the bidder undertakes to win at least three tricks.
Four - the bidder undertakes to win at least four tricks.
Nap (or Five) - the bidder undertakes to win all five tricks.
Wellington - the bidder undertakes to win all five tricks (same as Nap, but for a higher reward). Wellington can only be bid if another player has **pass, the hand is not** played, and the next dealer shuffles and deals.

Play
The high bidder leads to the first trick and the suit of this first card played by the bidder is trumps for the hand.

Players must follow suit if they can; a player who has no card of the suit led is free to play any card - either trumping or discarding from another suit.

Each trick is won by the highest trump in it, or if it contains no trumps, by the highest card of the suit led. The winner of each trick leads to the next.

Scoring
If the bidder is successful each of the other players pays the bidder depending on the bid:

Three: 3 units
Four: 4 units
Five (Nap): 5 units
Wellington: 10 units

If the bidder wins insufficient tricks, the bidder must pay each opponent the same amount that he would have won.

Variations
Additional bids are allowed by some groups as follows:

Two: A bid to win two tricks - if allowed this is the lowest bid, worth 2 units and ranking below Three.

Mis: A bid to lose every trick - it fails if the opponents can force the bidder to win a trick. It is worth 3 points and ranks between Three and Four in the bidding.

Blücher: A bid to win all five tricks. It can only be bid after another player has bid Wellington, and is worth 20 units.

Some players double the payment for Nap, Wellington or Blücher if they are won but not if they are lost. Some double them whether won or lost - paying 10 for Nap, 20 for Wellington and 40 for Blücher.

In the variation Purchase Nap, before the bidding each player may pay a fixed stake - typically 1 unit - to a pool, and discard any number of cards.

The dealer then gives the player an equal number of replacement cards from the undealt stock. The pool is won by the first player who bids Nap, Wellington or Blücher and wins five tricks.

RECIPES
Circa 1920

Rabbit Pudding with Mushrooms
Sufficient quantity for 4-6 persons
2 young rabbits
4-5 sage leaves
2-3 tablespoonfuls chopped onion
8 ounces (227 grams) mushrooms
salt and pepper
a few slices of fat bacon
8 ounces (227 grams) suet pastry

Line a 1 pint (0.47 litre) pudding basin with two thirds of the pastry, reserving the remaining third for the lid. Joint the rabbits and arrange a layer in the bottom of the basin. Sprinkle with a little sage and onion and then a layer of peeled mushrooms, seasoning and strips of bacon. Continue these layers until the basin is full. Three quarters fill the basin with water. Roll out the remaining pastry to cover the top and press it firmly in position. Cover with greased paper and steam for 3 to 4 hours. Serve with vegetables.

Devonshire Junket
1 quart (0.95 litre) new milk
nutmeg or cinnamon
1 wineglassful brandy or rum
powdered sugar
1 dessertspoonful rennet
Devonshire cream

Heat the milk until luke warm, then pour it into a junket or trifle dish. Stir in the rennet and brandy and keep stirring for a few minutes, then place in a warm spot until set. When cold sift sugar over and a little nutmeg or cinnamon and cover with a layer of Devonshire cream.

Brains on Toast
2 sets of brains
white stock
1 egg
vinegar
4 croutons of fried bread
breadcrumbs
8 rashers of bacon
lemon
parsley
frying fat

Always be careful that the brains are quite fresh. Let them lie for an hour in a basin of cold water, to which a teaspoonful of vinegar has been added. Remove the skins and put the brains in a saucepan with sufficient well-flavoured cold white stock to cover.
Bring to the boil, simmer gently for 10 minutes, then lift the brains out and let them get cold. Cut four croutons of bread the same size round as the brains and fry them a pale gold colour. When the brains are cold, dip them into whole beaten up egg and then into fine white breadcrumbs. Fry them a nice brown.
Roll and thread the bacon on skewers and while the brains are frying, put them in a tin, into a hot oven, and cook for two or three minutes.
Drain the brains and stand each one on a crouton of bread in a dish. Put the rolled bacon in the centre, and garnish with a few sprigs of either fried or fresh parsley and slices of lemon.

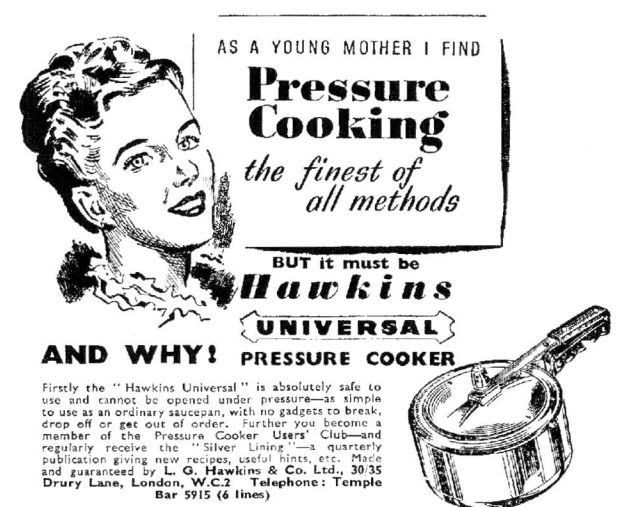

Grocery List

Malta 6th Jan 1939

3 lbs Flour	8d	(3p)
1 Doz Matches	3d	(1p)
4 ozs of Tobacco	2s 0 1/2d	(10p)
1 lb Lard	7d	(3p)
6 Cooking Eggs	4d	(2p)
6 Oxo	6 1/2d	(3p)
6 Fresh Eggs	11d	(5p)
Washing Sheets*	2d	(1p)
Life Insurance	1s 2d	(6p)
Owing	1s 6d	(7p)
Pocket money	2s	(10p)
Dress	1s	(5p)
Clothes	2s	(10p)
Vegetables	1s 6d	(7p)
Stamps	6d	(3p)
Fare	6d	(3p)
Total	15s 4d	(77p)

* A Maltese woman used to come around and wash sheets

All this would come from the NAAFI. As forces personnel we were not allowed to buy milk, cheese or butter from anywhere else because it could come from Goats and they'd eat anything.

Navy Food Slang

The British matelot has always been famed for his sense of humour in the face of adversity, particularly at the hands of naval cooks. A whole vocabulary has built up for the often served dishes. Here are a few of the more repeatable ones.

Spithead Pheasant	Kippers
Babies Heads	Tinned Steak & Kidney Pudding
Chinese Wedding Cake	Rice Pudding
365 (or Marines Breakfast)	Egg & Bacon
Arigonis	Tinned Tomatoes
Goffas	Fizzy Drink
Mrs B (Beeton)	Tinned 'Duff' (Sponge pudding)
Mad Dog's Vomit	Mixed Vegetable Salad
Cow Pie	Steak Pie
HITS	Herrings in Tomato Sauce
Cackle Berries	Boiled Eggs
Yellow Peril	Smoked Haddock
Elephants Footprints	Spam Fritters
Seggies	Grapefruit Segments
Jippers	Gravy

"Tala" ICING EQUIPMENT

for good results and easy work

There are 42 different tubes, making a delightful pattern, for you to choose from.

No. 1690 Icing Syringe in carton.

No. 1705 Icing Set as shown in carton.

Write for latest illustrated folder to:

"TALA" WORKS (DEPT. K). STOURBRIDGE, WORCS.

'You're RIGHT! — the Best Recipe DOES demand the Best Ingredients'

BEATALL TABLE JELLIES
BEATALL CUSTARD POWDER · BEATALL BLANCMANGE
BEATALL BATTER FLOUR · BEATALL SELF-RAISING FLOUR
HOMEFLAKE PLAIN FLOUR · BEATALL SEMOLINA
HOMEFLAKE SELF-RAISING FLOUR
BEATALL FAMOUS COCONUT CAKE MIXTURE
BEATALL FAMOUS SPONGE CAKE MIXTURE
BEATALL MADEIRA CAKE MIXTURE
MACARONI (16 Varieties)
LONG SPAGHETTI and VERMICELLI
BEATALL 'PREEMIX'

Insist on 'BEATALL'

J. GREEN'S 'BEATALL' FOOD PRODUCTS LTD.
WELLESLEY ROAD, LONDON, W.4. Tel. CHiswick 6415/7
Manufacturers of CEREOCA and other fine foods!

PAUL ROGERS

Following Hooe School Paul Rogers went to Plympton Grammar School and Newton Abbot Secondary School. He trained as an actor under Michael Chekhov at Dartington Hall and entered films on a small-time basis in 1932. Pauls' acting career began in earnest when he made his London stage debut in 1938.

Following war service in the Royal Navy he joined the Old Vic and went on to become a member of the Royal Shakespeare Company, establishing himself as a versatile Shakespearean actor, playing everything from Hamlet to Bottom. While at the Old Vic he met Rosalind Boxall who was also in the cast of 'Love's Labours Lost' at the New Theatre in 1949 and they married later.

A frequent visitor to Broadway he won a Tony award in 1967 for his performance in Harold Pinter's 'The Homecoming'.

His film roles include
William Pitt in Beau Brummel (1954)
Svengali (1955)
Irish journalist Frank Harris in Trial of Oscar Wilde (1960)
The Mark (1961)
Lt. Ratcliffe in Billy Budd (1962)
Stolen Hours (1963)
The Tenth Man (1988)

In 1987 he starred as the Dean in the Channel Four TV International Emmy Award winning dramatisation by Malcolm Bradbury of Tom Sharpe's hilarious novel Porterhouse Blue, together with David Jason, Ian Richardsn, Charles Gray, John Sessions and Griff Rhys-Jones. In my opinion there is no better nor more delightful example of an ex pupil of Hooe School at work. This is available on DVD published by Channel 4.

EDWIN ROGERS

Paul Rogers has kindly contributed the following affectionate acount of his father.

Edwin Rogers. Born 1890 in what must have been a brand new terrace house in Laira Bridge Road, Plymouth.

He was the eldest of eight children of William, a country carpenter from Holbeton, (eight miles down the Kingsbridge road and who became a superintendent of Plymouth Police and Captain of the Fire Brigade) and Elizabeth Grose, a Cornish woman from near Mevagissey.

Edwin attended Prince Rock Boy's School and, thanks to the Headmaster's foresight, he was among the first pupils at the new Plymouth Grammar School. While at school he came under the influence of a charismatic young curate of St Simon's Church, Plymouth, who later in life became the Suffragan Bishop of Crediton. At Bible class he [Edwin] met and fell in love with my mother, Dulcie Myrtle Collier. He also formed a great desire to enter the Church, an ambition sensibly stepped on by my authoritarian Grandfather. Instead Edwin went to St Paul's Church of England Teacher Training College, Cheltenham and became the schoolmaster still remembered with affection and gratitude by a few surviving people of my age.

He was assistant master at Plympton Public School at the time of his appointment to Hooe C of E Primary School. It was a good day for him and the school; that bright summer day in 1922 when we moved to the schoolhouse, Hooe. As you suggest the school was out of control. A very rough element, mainly from Turnchapel, had broken the spirit of three supply headmasters. Unlike these less than happy men Edwin was able to grasp the nettle - take the bull by the horns - what you will. He was one of them (the intake at Prince Rock included many similar young people) and he served as an example of what could be achieved with luck and application.

Edwin was a disciplinarian of a type frowned upon by today's goody-goodies. He couldn't shut the door on the problem and leave it to someone else. He always possessed a cane. I once witnessed such a purchase and I was impressed by the great care he took in its selection. It was as thick as my little finger now and, arriving home, the first thing he did was to take his pocket knife and cut off the fancy hook handle leaving both ends serviceable.

In fact it spent most of its life lying along the front edge of his desk. My father caned but was never a flogger. He took no pleasure in the exercise and once accomplished the slate was wiped clean. He caned according to strict rules. I'm an expert because I was caned for swearing at Vanny Grey [see the photo on page 6].

The malefactor stood straight and took his punishment like the man many of the boys almost were at fourteen. The right hand was extended at right angles to the body and received from one to five strokes meaningfully administered. The same was dealt to the left hand. One tucked both hands into one's armpits for comfort.

In fact he loved the spirit in the boys which made them rebellious, as he did the particular awareness of the children from the Army married quarters at [Forts] Stamford and Bovisand. When he left their sea-port hardiness for the softer mid-Devon he missed the quality.

After ten very successful years at Hooe he was appointed to Highweek Senior School, a large school on the outskirts of Newton Abbot. Here he caned for one thing only: bullying. From his room overlooking the playgrounds his one good eye made sure no-one got away with this most loathsome practice.

He was offered further advancement as Head of a large school in Exeter but by then Dulcie had a whole life centred round the church, the town and a wide circle of friends. To avoid her distress Edwin very happily stayed where he was until his retirement. He then continued to serve as temporary Head until the post was eventually and satisfactorily filled.

They retired to 7 Western Terrace, Collins's Road; a little house in a row under Totnes Castle where Dulcie pre deceased Edwin by ten years. They are buried in the beautiful Highweek Churchyard on the hill outside Newton Abbot.

The Schoolhouse and top right the school. 2003.

HOOE SCHOOL

Hooe School was operated on two sites until 1931 when the replacement buildings were completed on Penny Park field at the Southern end of Hooe Lake. Up to that time children aged 5 yrs up to 7 yrs attended the infants section, which was held in two rooms at the shore end of the Turnchapel ferry pier. The seniors, from 7 to 14, went to what is now St John's Church Hall at the top of Church Hill.

Just after the first world war the school was in poor shape. It had no permanent Head teacher, the staff were under considerable stress and lacked support and the children were underachieving because of a succession of uncommitted temporary head teachers. Reasons for frequent absences by the children included Diphtheria, Measles, TB, throat infections and inclement weather. The latter may seem a bit feeble but when you consider that all the children walked some distance to school and the facilities for drying wet clothes at school were poor then rough weather would be a severe deterrent to attendance. It appears that a significant number of children came from poor families, suffered from learning difficulties had a lack of self discipline and were generally prone to ringworm and head lice. These extracts from the school logbook for the time illustrate some of the problems the school faced.

October 7th 1919

During the Great War the school premises were required and used by the military authorities for a military hospital. The children attended Plymstock, Oreston and Turnchapel infant schools during the period. The school was recommenced on October 7th 1919.
92 children present.
Staff: W Westcott commenced temporary duties as Headteacher.
Miss England in charge of Standards 1 and 2,

October 10th 1919

Mrs Marshall commenced duties and took charge of standards 3 and 4.

A constant thread running through the early parts of the log is that one of the teachers, Miss England, was particularly erratic in attendance and punctuality, sometimes with reasons of ill health, lateness and missing the train but often with no reason recorded. She seems to have left around the 2nd June 1922 as no further mention is made of her and yet her departure is not recorded and another teacher is appointed.

October 20th 1920

Report

The present Headmaster, who is on the unattached staff of the authority, took charge of this department when it returned to its own premises on the 6th October 1919. Soon after this one of the two assistant teachers left and for nine weeks no-one was sent in her place.

After due allowance has been made for the natural backwardness of some of the children and for the unprepared condition of those presented from the Infants Department it cannot be said that satisfactory progress is being made. The Head Teacher fully realises that the attainments of his pupils are very low but he has failed to adapt the work to their needs with the result that the children are often set exercises which are beyond them and which they only manage to do with much help from their teachers. They are not being trained to master their own difficulties. Moreover no arrangements are made for those scholars who spend four years in the top group to make progress in any subject except arithmetic. The Headmaster and the teacher of the middle group appear to lack persistency and are too easily satisfied, with the inevitable result that work is carelessly done.

The teacher of the lowest class is young and inexperienced and needs more guidance. The discipline is not good. There is some unsteadiness and inattention while some of the scholars are inclined to copy their neighbour's work. The tests given in composition and arithmetic at the visit were badly done and even the best children read with little expression and with slovenly pronunciation while in each class there are some very backward children who show little or no ability in attacking new words.

The present condition of the school is very disturbing. It is hoped that arrangements will soon be made for a permanent Headteacher and that a determined effort will be made to improve the work. The attention of the manager is called to article 3 of schedule 4 of the code.

Buildings

This report is written at the request of the local education authority. These premises, which consist of one large room and a small classroom, possess several defects, are separated by a wooden partition which reaches only half way to the roof and at one end there is a low gallery. Both the rooms are badly lighted and ventilated. There are only two windows in the classroom. One of which, 3 ft 6 ins by 3 ft 6 ins, swings, contains leaded glass and is at a height of 6 ft 6 ins. The other, 4 ft by 10 ft is fitted with dim glass although it overlooks the playground. The ventilation is by means of one roof ventilator, a swing leaded window and a small swing window fitted at the top of the other window. There is no low inlet.

The main room is lighted by one small and two large leaded windows and two dormer windows. The former are at a height of six foot and the latter twelve feet. There are four roof ventilators, one swing window in each of the dormer windows and one small swing window in each of the large leaded windows. While the girls offices are immediately below one of these. Here again there are no low inlets. The heating is by means of closed stoves one of which is fixed in one corner of the main room. There no fire guards. All the doors open inwards.

The cloakroom is a porch in front of the school. It is divided in two by a wooden partition which does not reach the roof. There are leaded windows. The only means of ventilation is by means of the doors and the very small space between the roof and the top of the wall. The majority of the pegs are missing from the boys cloakroom.

The offices are close to the school and the girls' can only be reached by passing through the main room. The closets are on the trough system and are automatically flushed. The urinal is very small being an open rectangular space three foot six wide.

January 17th 1921

Children who attended Bovisand Military school now attend this school.

January 31st 1921

I have taken temporary charge of this school today. Number on books 105. Number present 97. Signed Edwin J Barnicott.

June 10th 1921

Edwin J Barnicott finished his temporary duties.

June 13th 1921

Francis A Mortimore, unattached supply staff, takes over temporary charge of the school.
I have today completed a week as temporary head

teacher. I find the children for the greater part in a very backward condition. They lack concentration and are listless and apathetic. Only a very few displaying any keenness or taking any pride in their work.

By all accounts Miss England and Miss Clark did not get on. She was the junior and Miss England gave her unpleasant jobs to do such as clearing out a cupboard that contained medical supplies and bottled specimens from when the building had been a hospital in the first world war. Miss Clark later married Reg Coleman.

June 23rd 1921
The school did not meet today, a special holiday having been granted to commemorate the recent visit the HRH the Prince of Wales to this county.

Hooe St Johns' Church Hall 2003.
(Previously Hooe School).
Rear elevation showing the kitchen block that was added circa 1920 owing to the increasing number of pupils who required school lunches.

July 13th 1921
Date of inspection: July 13th 1921
Scholars on books 118
Scholars present at inspection: Boys 55 Girls 55
Withdrawn from all religious instruction: nil
Withdrawn from only part of instruction: nil
Teacher responsible for Group 1 Miss A Clarke, Group 2 Miss A G England, Group 3 Mr Mortimore

The changing staff has militated against the successful teaching of this school during the past year. Some of the children, however, answered with intelligence and interest indicating that good instruction has been given. It is to be hoped that a permanent Headteacher will soon be appointed as the filling of such an appointment by supply for such a long period cannot be educationally in the interests of the children.

Considerable praise is due to the headmaster and his two loyal and enthusiastic assistants, all of whom have been in the school for less than a twelvemonth, for the remarkable improvement that has taken place in the condition of this department, which was previously very unsatisfactory. Much thought has been spent by the Headteacher on the preparation of the syllabus and his supervision is effective while some success is accompanying his efforts to arouse the parent's interest in the school. The more enlightened methods of teaching have awakened new interests in the scholars who enter zest into all their work as is partly shown in the pride they take in all their written exercises, which were formally characterized by much carelessness. At the present juncture it is inadvisable to report in detail on the work especially as the teachers are fully aware of the shortcomings and are endeavouring to remedy them. Mention, however, must be made of the marked progress in singing and physical exercises and also of the care that is taken in ascertaining the effectiveness of the carefully prepared and stimulating oral lessons by means of some form of self expression, in the case of the younger pupils, and written tests in the upper classes.

It is confidently felt that in time this will become a thoroughly good school. Beyond the removal of the gallery nothing has been done to remedy the defects in the premises pointed out in the report of 1920.

October 28th 1921
Miss England not present at opening of school in the morning. She arrived at 9:20 and remained for the morning session but was not well enough to stay for afternoon school.

January 10th 1922
I took charge of the school today on its reassembling after the Christmas Holidays.
Walter Light,
unattached supply staff, Devon County Education Committee

March 27th 1922
Mrs Mabel Beatrice Redstone commenced duty on a supply basis.
April 12th 1922
Possibly Miss England terminated her employment on this date or on June 2nd at the Whitsun holidays.

May 23rd 1922

At about 9:30 this morning during a thunderstorm the school was struck by lightning and a portion of the roof at the northern end of the main room was playground. The electric current apparently passed along the gas pipe leading from the meter to the roof and in its passage also shattered and threw down some of the inner wooden lining of the roof shattered.

Fortunately no-one was injured though, naturally, the children were very much frightened by the terrific crash caused by the lightning. The Rev F Gilbertson was quickly on the spot and with me made a thorough examination of the building to ascertain the full extent of the damage and to make sure that the lightning had not started a smouldering fire which might lead to a conflagration. Such, however, was not the case and later on we were able to resume our work.

June 2nd 1922
My term of duty was terminated today.
Walter Light.

June 12th 1922
My duties as permanent headmaster commenced today. School and Staff divided:
Years 1 and 2: Mrs M Redstone (temporary)
Year 3: Miss Turner (supply staff)
Years 4, 5 and 6 Edwin Rogers (Headmaster)

June 17th 1922
Miss Alice Clark terminated her engagement here today.

August 28th 1922
Miss N Knott replaced Miss Turner.

Hooe School, now Hooe St John's Church Hall, in 2003

Interior looking NWest. Where the ceiling joins the walls at the left, far end, is where the lightning strike penetrated. The small door at the end opens onto a narrow stone stairway (below) that led to the boys' playground and toilets at the rear.

Left: Interior looking SEast. Main entrance on the right. The cloakrooms ran along the opposite side of the right hand wall to another door at the far end. The doorway on the left leads to the present kitchen area.

George Siggers

Since completing the first edition of this book I have been intrigued by the appearance of pupil No 12, George Siggers, in the Hooe School photograph on page 8. He seemed rather out of place. Well dressed compared to his classmates and with a slightly superior pose and expression. I wondered who he was but I did not pursue it.

Eight years later I was mentioning this in passing to Debbie Watson, of the Plymouth & West Devon Record Office and much to my surprise and delight, she discovered who he and his family were. The details from the records gave more clues and leads for a fascinating story.

George W Siggers' father was William George Siggers, born in Battersea in 1887, the only son of a carpenter/joiner. He left school at the age of 11 or 12 and joined a firm of solicitors as a clerk.

In August 1904 William enlisted for three years Army service with the 31st company Heavy Battery, Royal Garrison Artillery and this was extended to nine years reserve service.

He met Annie Maude Brown, the daughter of a labourer, who was born in Turnchapel and whose family lived at 9 Clovelly View. They were married in 1909 at Wandsworth. Their first child, William Frederick J Siggers, was born a year later in 1910 and registered in Woolwich.

William Snr. was promoted to Bombardier and posted to France in 1914. Annie was pregnant and with her husband abroad on war service she came home to Turnchapel. In 1914 their second son George was born and registered at Hooe.

William survived his time in France and rose to the rank of Sergeant by 1917, when he returned home to London. He was discharged on the 31st of January 1919.

In November 1920 the whole family emigrated to Canada, sailing from Southampton to Quebec then by train across Canada to Vancouver then by steamship to Britannia Beach, where William had a job at the Britannia Copper Mine.

They stayed for five years then in April 1925 they returned to 9 Clovelly View, Turnchapel. The reason is not known. William is now referred to as a Mill Operator. George attends Hooe School and has his photograph taken, probably in October 1925.

This was, and still is, the most common time to take school photographs to record the new intakes and classes. Some were also taken in June to record the final year children about to leave. The children would have been told of the occasion and to dress smartly. George, if correctly identified, also appears in the whole school photo on page 11 where he is dressed more like his classmates.

His father, William, stays for seven months then returns to Canada in November 1925. Leaving from Liverpool.

In July 1926 his wife Annie with sons William and George leave Southampton on the RMS Ascania bound for Quebec to join him at Britannia Beach. At this time Annie is 37, William (described as a machinist) is 16 and George, 11 or 12, is a scholar.

RMS Ascania (Cunard)

He would be going back to a country the wonders of which he would have told his friends in Hooe and Turnchapel. He must have been an interesting and exotic fellow pupil, who having been in Canada for five years would have a Canadian accent.

I contacted the curator of the mining museum. It seems that George eventually worked in the mine and married a woman called Rhoda, she died in 2002, George had died earlier.   *Robin Blythe-Lord*

Britannia Beach in 2010 with the Britannia Copper Mine climbing up the opposite hillside.

Index

A

AA sign 47
Aldershot 43
Alvington Road 44
Artisan Dwellings 17
Astor, Lady 18
Australian airmen 37
Avondale Terrace 4

B

Battle of Britain 36
Bayly's timber yard 48
Beach Cottage 5, 6
Berkertex 38
Bill Cox 25, 45
Blackshirts 51
Blood on the Sands of Tunisia 40
Bovisand 12, 47
Brains on Toast 63
Brenda Puleston 38
Britannia Beach 70
Britannia Copper Mine 70

C

Canada 70
Cattewater 5
Cavill, Caroline Emma Ann Caple 4
Childhood highlights 12
Chilwell 42
Cinemas 57
City Mission Band 15
City Silver Band 15
Courting and Marriage 25
Cucklington 34, 36
Cycling accident 18

D

Dalmeny House 57
Dartington Hall 65
Defiance Clothing Works 23
Devonport 4, 5
Devonshire Junket 63
Dragonara Palace 30

E

Eady, Dorothy 58
Eady, Reuben 58
Eddie Hunwicks 47
Eddystone buses 15
Edwin Rogers 65

Electric Cinema, The 57
Empire Electric cinema 23

F

Fanshawe Terrace 34, 41
FED 35mm camera 38
Flit 31
Flying Boats 60
Food 7
Forth Bridge 4
Frank Rogers 50

G

George Siggers 70
Glacial acetic acid 22
Goulds 17
Granby Barracks 32
Greenwich school 51

H

Harwoods, bakers 49
Heath and Reach 36, 37
Hele Terrace 45
Herbert Hunwicks 45
Hexton Woods 47
Highweek Senior School 66
HMS Fisguard 53
HMT Dunera 61
HMT Lancashire 33
Holbrook 51
Hooe 5, 33, 34, 35, 37
Hooe and Turnchapel school 47
Hooe Chapel Outing 16
Hooe Lake 5, 6, 14, 48
Hooe Lake Quarry 48
Hooe School 1, 2, 8, 12, 51
Hooe Schoolhouse 66
Hooe School, inspector's report 67
Hoosh Teegoosh 7, 49
Hunwicks, Herbert Henry 4

I

Incendiary bombs 53

J

Jennycliff 47
Jeromes Photographers 23
Jolliffe, Rene 13

K

Keyham 4
Kodak 44

L

Lash up and Stow 49
Leica 38
Lightning strike 8

M

Malta 4, 30
Malta grocery list 64
Manor Road 37, 44
Mice 43
Milk round 9, 50
Milk Round 50
Mount Batten 37, 60

N

NAP Card game 62
Navy food slang 64
New Palladium, The 58
Nits 50
Notte Street 17
Nottingham 42
Nursery Pomade 50

O

Oil tank fire 53

P

Palace Saloon buses 15
Paper round 50
Paul Rogers 65
Photography in Plymouth 60
Plasterdown Camp 43
Plymouth 2, 4, 12, 15, 16, 32
Plympton Grammar School 65
Plympton Public School 65
Post war years 42
Prince Rock Boy's School 65

R

RAAF 60
Rabbit Pudding with Mushrooms 63
Radford Castle 14
Radford caves 47
Radford Duckponds 14
Radford House 14
Recipes c1920 63
Reckitt, Isaac 54
Regent Cinema 24
Regent Cinema, The 59
Rogers, Edwin 8, 65
Rogers, Paul 8, 65
Royal Hospital School 52
Royal Oak 6

S

Scotland 5
Sewage 55
Sicily 39
Siggers, George 70
Sloe Gin 12, 56
Somerset Depot 42
Somerset Light Infantry 40
South Queensferry 4
SS Moreton Bay 30
Staddon Brakes 6
St Georges' Bay 31, 32
St. George's Bay 30
Sticky Dinner 49
St John's Church Hall 47
St Levan's Road School 23
St Maurice 45
St Maurice Tenant's Association 45
Stone barges 48
Stuart Photo Services 44
Stuart's Photo Services 17
Stuarts Photo Services 46
Sunday School 12
Sunlight soap 50
Swanage 36
Swift Studios 23, 34, 36

T

Taunton 42, 44
The Bird Cage 31
The Chocolate Kid 26
The Palace Theatre 25
Timber rafts 48
Toe-Rag 7
Topsham 42
Turnchapel and Oreston Ferry 15

W

War Damage Claims Office 53
Washday 54
Wash house 6
Welwyn Garden City 37
Western National 43, 44
West Huntspill 4
William Friese-Green 60
Winter work 23
Work and Marriage 17